KV-000-350

MERCURIO'S MENU

MERCURIO'S MENU

Paul Mercurio's travel stories and recipes from the popular TV show

MURDOCH BOOKS

CONTENTS

People often look at me with surprise and ask me why, when, where and how I got into food, let alone have my own food show on television. The truth is, whilst I can chart how it all happened I am still somewhat surprised, perplexed and very happy that it did.

Without going through my family history, somewhere along the way I developed not just a love of food but also a love of cooking. I put it down to the fact that ever since I was a young boy I have always been a performer and a large part of being a performer is about being creative. Having a love of food is a good place to begin the journey into diverse and fulfilling food experiences, along with the understanding that food is about creativity and the ability to express your personality. Just look at all the rock star chefs we have on television now, they are all about expressing themselves and their art. I have done this all my life through dance, choreography, acting and now, through my cooking — and don't I feel lucky!

My very first TV cooking appearance was back in the mid-seventies when I appeared on the Helen O'Grady show making a toasted cheese sandwich — the perfect after-school snack. Helen O'Grady was one of my first drama teachers at John Curtin Theatre Arts High School, a rather out-there lady who wore very large jewellery, had big hair, wore lots of make-up and just happened to have her own afternoon kids show on TV in Perth, Western Australia. I am horrified to remember that I used single sliced and wrapped processed cheese which melted under the studio lights. Thankfully I have moved on from that.

My next foodie experience was when I scored a job at my local Red Rooster outlet. Red Rooster is a chicken chain serving up the usual fare of roast chicken, chips, peas, gravy, corn and I was their new head chef at the ripe old age of 16. Yep, for $1.45 per hour I cooked, cleaned and served up everything. Looking back on it now it amounted to slave labour but I also learnt how to work hard, respect my ingredients and have integrity in my work. One of the best things about the job was back in those days (late seventies) when I made the chicken rolls, I would use the left over chickens from the day before. As there was no meat on the wings they were supposed to be discarded but I would fill up bags of them and keep them in the fridge. Then at the end of the night I would make sure to cook extra chips just in case we had a late run for them. At the end of the night my mum and I would go home with a couple of bags of hot chips and cold wings to a house full of friends waiting for a feast.

One of the managers at the store when I started was a Bangladeshi guy called Gerry who left Red Rooster to start his own place cooking traditional Bangladeshi and Indian food. I used to go down to his market stall and help him cook and serve customers on weekends. During this time I also met a Chinese martial arts instructor,

Jonny, who also had a stall at the markets. I became friends with him, often hanging out at his stall helping where I could with cooking or serving. At the time, I was a full-time student with the Western Australian Ballet Company and Jonny, in between cooking and prepping food, would give me special Chinese liniments to help with sore, strained and often torn muscles. These guys were great as they had a passion for their traditional food and a desire to share that with people, they opened my eyes and taste buds to world cuisine. They also had a great zest for life and it seemed to me that their food brought them joy — cooking and sharing was as necessary and natural as breathing. I would like to think that this was their gift to me.

Mum was a good cook but as we were a family of five living on a single income, there really was not a lot of room to play with ingredients or to get too fancy. We used to eat a lot of lamb, or I should say mutton, as Mum would buy a side of lamb for a pretty cheap price and we would diligently eat our way through it. I love lamb but to this day my brother and sister have difficulty sitting down to a meal of it.

When I left home and moved to Melbourne to study at the Australian Ballet School, I got a job working at Taco Bill, a Mexican restaurant. I started out making the dips and the salads, which was fun and I was about to be promoted to the ovens but alas my dance studies were suffering and I had to give my nightly cooking career away. However, being away from home meant cooking every meal for myself and thus began my journey into produce, experiments, burnt toast, weird concoctions, the odd bout of food poisoning and the power of cooking a romantic dinner. I am happy to say I am still on this journey but have left the food poisoning bit back in the depths of the eighties.

I was a dancer with the Sydney Dance Company, and spent ten years travelling the world, which for a foodie was just wonderful. I loved performing in different countries and even more so, discovering the foods of those countries. I never understood how some members of the troupe could eat out at a typical fast-food joint we have back at home instead of a restaurant to try the local cuisine. When I started doing films, I was lucky enough to make movies in a range of countries and had the opportunity to really sample the regional culture and food. I learned that the food in L.A., Texas and New York is as different to one another as the food of Northern and Southern Italy. I love these contrasts and find them both inspiring and exciting.

Being an actor in Australia is a tough gig and whether you like it or not, periods of award-winning work can be followed by dark, angst-filled periods of no work. What does one do with all that spare time and creative energy? If you are like me, you cook. I started making my own sourdough breads, sausages, salamis, beer and smoked meats. I dabbled in French cuisine, Thai food, Tex Mex, Spanish, Italian, Chinese, Barbecue, slow-braising, wok-cooking, and more. I made beer ice cream, beer sorbet, beer sausages even a beer cheese cake — as you may have noticed, I love beer. In short, I cooked with no rules or guidelines, I played around, had fun and in doing so, discovered what cooking is all about.

Throughout my life and work, food has been a great source of interest, creativity, passion, inspiration and occasionally income but I still haven't answered the question of how I ended up with my own food show. The simple answer is luck.

Perhaps from watching too many cooking shows and from doing a few cooking segments on TV myself, I thought it would be cool to be a TV-cooking-bloke. One day I read in the paper that Channel 7 were looking for a host for a new food show. I did everything I could to find out all about it hoping to get an audition but it was to no avail. Then one Friday afternoon a producer I had been working with rang me and mentioned that he was

doing the new food show. Unfortunately for me he had developed the show for a particular chef so I was out of the picture. Early the next morning, I received a phone call from that same producer explaining he was down at the Melbourne Food and Wine Festival with a crew ready to shoot the pilot but the chef had inexplicably pulled out of the show. Since he had no host, he asked whether would I come down and fill in — of course, I said yes. Half an hour later I was hosting the show — interviewing wonderful food producers and tasting some great food. Upon watching the pilot and seeing some of my other TV food presentations, the producer, the sponsors and the network decided I could have the gig. Am I glad that chef pulled out!

That show was called *The Food Trail*. We shot six episodes in Victoria in 2005 and four in Tasmania in 2006, it was shown nationally on Channel 7 and rated very well. A year after we shot the last episode of *The Food Trail* a different production company — WTFN — developed *Mercurio's Menu* and the rest is history.

This book features recipes from series one and two as well as recipes from the various talented chefs who appeared on the show. People often ask me where I get my recipes from and the simple answer is, I make them up. The great thing about the show is that it is produce-

driven so my task is to work out something interesting to do with the produce I am filming. Sometimes a recipe will just pop into my head and other times I will rack my brains, look through all of my cookbooks and trawl the internet for clues as to how other people may have used the particular food item. I will then play around with my ideas, build a recipe then cook it and see if it works. Quite often when I make a dish on camera it is the first time I have cooked it and my fingers are crossed that it will work. So far I haven't had a disaster!

I hope you enjoy cooking the recipes from this book. Think of the recipes as guidelines — sure, cook them as they are written but don't be afraid to make changes according to your own taste.

Add a bit more of this, or a little less of that when and where you want, and don't forget to write down what you do so that you can re-create it and continue to hone the recipe to your liking.

Personally, I love to write with a pencil in my cookbooks, it's kind of irreverent and naughty but at the same time freeing and fun. And that's what cooking is all about — being creative, nourishing the soul as well as the body and sharing the joy with family and friends.

Cheers!

NEW SOUTH WALES

I found a wonderful synergy between producer, craftsman, cook and chef – they care passionately about the produce, where it comes from and where it goes. Travelling around New South Wales, I realised just how lucky a country we are.

The view was sensational, the restaurant one of Sydney's acclaimed and the chef a master craftsman when it comes to all things food. And here I was, a home cook at best trying out a dish I had only ever cooked once before for my wife and hoping that I wouldn't stuff it up. I looked over at the chef as I delicately folded the crabmeat within the fresh piece of yellow fin tuna. There was a look in his eye and a smile on his face but I wasn't sure if it was the look someone gives a child who is trying their best even though they had it all wrong or if it was because he was impressed. Thankfully it was the latter! Yes, I cooked for and impressed Robert Marchetti a leading Two Hatted chef and restaurateur, I was happy and relieved. The restaurant was Icebergs in the world-renowned suburb of Bondi. New South Wales has an abundance of wonderful fresh produce and it also has an array of absolutely terrific restaurants and chefs who very generously allowed me into their kitchens and quite patiently let me to cook for them. I made turkey and wild rice stuffed sweet peppers with a tomato, chocolate and chilli sauce for a chef in Byron Bay — he said they were 'surprisingly good' — that's a compliment isn't it? I cooked a snail and yabbie pie for a French chef in the Hunter Valley — he offered me a job. I invited all the producers from one area to lunch and cooked their produce for them — a very nerve-racking experience — but very rewarding when they all loved the way I used their products.

I could go on about the quality of the produce, the fabulous oranges that Betty grows, the goats that Norma and Colin love and hate to part with, the beer Luke and Keith make, the fresh plump snails Robert and Helen are so fond of, the amazing organic spatchcock that Ray and Kerry lovingly raise, the avocados Robyn and Henry produce, Helmut's weird and wonderful exotic fruits, Matthew's Sunforest free-range turkeys, Brent and Jennifer's traditional sourdough, Lyle and Karen's honey, Barefoot Buck's native finger limes…to name just a few.

Let's face it, the quality and variety of produce in New South Wales is amazing, as are the people that take that produce and with passion, care and commitment and make it into something so mouth-wateringly tempting that you have to buy it and eat it. Carol's laksa recipe is a great example of this, as are Kaz's smallgoods and the custard tarts that Fernando has been making for 35 years — sadly they are not in this book as it is a treasured family recipe!

Pork and mushroom pot stickers

SERVES 4 AS A STARTER

For the filling: mix together all the ingredients in a large bowl.

Lay out a won ton wrapper and place a teaspoon of the filling along the middle on the diagonal, that is from one corner to the opposite. Have a small bowl of water nearby, then dab your finger in the water and moisten the four sides of the wrapper. Take opposite corners of the wrapper and stick them together, then lift the whole won ton by the stuck-together corner and, using your other hand, press the remaining openings closed. Put the pot sticker down, making sure to press it gently on the work surface so that it sits on a flat bottom with the top corner pointing up to the sky. Repeat with the remaining wrappers and filling.

Cook the pot stickers in batches by heating 1 tablespoon of oil in a non-stick frying pan or wok (that has a tight-fitting lid). (Do not use too much oil to fry or the pot stickers will be too oily after they have steamed.) Place the pot stickers in the pan, flat bottom down, and fry for 2–3 minutes until golden brown. Pour in 125 ml (4 fl oz/½ cup boiling water and then cover with a lid and cook until all the water has evaporated, approximately 6–8 minutes. This finishes off the cooking of the pot stickers by boiling and steaming them.

Fry and boil in batches of 8 and keep the first batch warm whilst you cook the second batch.

Remove from the pan and put on a plate. Serve with a small side bowl of soy sauce and one of hot chilli sauce.

FILLING

250 g (9 oz) minced (ground) pork

50 g (1¾ oz/1 cup) thinly sliced Chinese cabbage (wong bok)

80 g (2¾ oz/½ cup) water chestnuts, rinsed, drained and chopped

100 g (3½ oz) mixed mushrooms (use a mix of black fungus, chestnut mushroom, shimeji and enoki), finely chopped

1 teaspoon grated fresh ginger

1 tablespoon soy sauce

2 teaspoons hoisin sauce

¼ teaspoon ground long pepper (see note)

¼ teaspoon ground mountain pepperleaf (see note)

¼ teaspoon salt

16 square won ton wrappers (the yellow ones made with egg)

vegetable or peanut oil, for frying

soy sauce and hot chilli sauce, to serve

Long pepper is an Indonesian pepper — the aroma is sweet, fragrant and musk-like and the flavour is similarly musky and peppery. Ground mountain pepperleaf has warm peppery notes combined with a delicate, eucalypt-like flavour.

Wild scallops with watercress and radish salad

RECIPE BY ROBERT MARCHETTI FROM ICEBERGS, BONDI

SERVES 4 AS A STARTER

12 wild scallops, on the shell (see note)

1 large green chilli, seeded and thinly sliced

2 garlic cloves, finely chopped

2 tablespoons extra virgin olive oil

4 cherry tomatoes, cut into 4 mm (⅛ inch) thick slices

1 bunch watercress, picked

3 radishes, sliced into matchsticks

90 ml (3 fl oz) lemon dressing

LEMON DRESSING

1½ garlic cloves

2 teaspoons salt

1½ tablespoons dijon mustard

1 tablespoon red wine vinegar

1 tablespoon lemon juice

4 tablespoons extra virgin oil

Preheat the oven to 200°C (400°F/Gas 6). For the dressing: Use a mortar and pestle to crush the garlic with the salt and mustard to form a paste. Add the vinegar and lemon juice and then the oil. Do not emulsify.

Cut the scallop from the shell, keeping the shells. Clean the scallops of the small muscle located at the bottom of the scallop, then return each scallop to its shell.

Mix together the chilli, garlic and olive oil. Spoon a generous amount onto the scallops, place slices of tomato on each scallop, season with salt and pepper, then place the scallops onto a baking tray. Bake for 5–6 minutes until just cooked.

Combine the watercress, radish matchsticks and a generous amount of the lemon dressing in a bowl.

Once the scallops are cooked, remove from the oven and serve immediately with the salad. Place a little watercress on the plate underneath the shells (to stop the shells sliding).

Wild scallops are available seasonally from Tasmania however you can also use farmed scallops as a substitute, which are available all year round.

Weed filo

RECIPE BY LIS BASTIAN FROM HER KITCHEN GARDEN, BLUE MOUNTAINS

SERVES 6

olive oil

1 onion, finely diced

1 garlic clove, finely chopped

1 small chilli, thinly sliced

2 cups of finely chopped weeds, greens and herbs — any combination of dandelion leaves, dock, plantain, sorrel, nasturtium, fennel, red mustard, kale, silverbeet (Swiss chard), chives, garlic chives, mint, dill, parsley, salad burnett, beetroot (beet) and broccoli greens

250 g (9 oz) Jannei goat's cheese (or your favourite brand), roughly chopped

2 eggs, beaten

20 sheets of filo pastry

melted butter, for brushing

Preheat the oven to 200°C (400°F/Gas 6). Heat a splash of oil in a frying pan and gently sweat the onion. When translucent, add the garlic and chilli and cook for several minutes. Add the weeds, greens and herbs, mixing through the cooked onion until well combined, and gently cook until the leaves are wilted.

Remove the pan from the heat and transfer everything to a bowl. Once cool, add the goat's cheese, beaten egg and some freshly ground pepper and a little salt.

Lay out 2 sheets of filo pastry on top of one another, brush with melted butter and repeat, 2 sheets at a time, until you have a stack of 10 sheets. Spread half the herb and cheese mixture along the long side of the pastry, then roll up. Make a second roll in the same way, using the rest of the pastry and filling.

Place the weed rolls on a baking tray, brush the top of each roll with melted butter and bake until the pastry looks golden brown.

Lis's garden really is an inspiration. She has turned her backyard into a food lover's paradise, not only growing a terrific variety of vegetables but also keeping her own bantam chooks for eggs. As she says, weeds are an important part of the garden structure and also, it seems, in the kitchen!

My experimental sichuan pork scroll

Make a hot water dough by combining the flours with a pinch of salt and then gradually add the boiling water to the flour, mixing until a dough forms. Turn out on to a floured bench or work surface and knead for 10 minutes, then set aside to rest.

Season the pork mince with a pinch of salt. Dry-fry the sichuan peppercorns in a small frying pan until they begin to lightly smoke and smell fragrant. Crush the sichuan peppercorns and the Chinese five-spice using a mortar and pestle and mix together.

Pour some sesame oil onto the bench. Roll half of the dough out into a long sausage. Now press it down to flatten it and use a rolling pin to stretch it out, turning it over as you do so and adding more sesame oil to the bench as needed to keep the dough pliant and to prevent it from sticking to the bench. Make a rectangle that is about 50 cm (20 inches) long and 8 cm (3¼ inches) wide.

Using half the pork, place in a line lengthways along the middle of the dough from one end to the other. Sprinkle half the spring onions and half the five-spice mix over the pork. Take one of the long edges of dough and fold it over the meat so that the dough touches the dough on the other side of the meat.

Fold the second long edge of dough up slightly over the overlapping dough and press together to seal. Do this all the way along so that you end up with a long thin sausage. Seal each end closed and tightly roll the sausage into a spiral shape. Lay this flat and then gently bash this disc with the flat of your hand so that it flattens and spreads. Don't worry if you split the dough a little. The disc should be about 16 cm (6¼ inches) across or so. Repeat with the remaining dough and filling.

Shallow-fry the discs in peanut oil — turning once. If you have flattened it out well it should cook through in 8–10 minutes. Sometimes I finish mine in a 180°C (350°F/Gas 4) oven for 5 minutes just to make sure the pork is cooked through.

Serve topped with chopped spring onions and bowls of soy sauce and chilli sauce on the side for dipping.

125 g (4½ oz/1 cup) plain (all-purpose) flour
125 g (4½ oz/1 cup) self-raising flour
125–185 ml (4–6 fl oz/½–¾ cup) boiling water
200 g (7 oz) minced (ground) pork
1–2 teaspoons sichuan peppercorns
½ teaspoon Chinese five-spice
sesame oil
4 spring onions (scallions), chopped
vegetable or peanut oil
chopped spring onion (scallion), extra, to serve
soy sauce and chilli sauce, to serve

I had a beautiful, fragrant fried flat bun stuffed with pork and spices when I was in Beijing. I loved it so much I went to the little shop that made them every day. When I came home I decided to have a go at making them for myself. My version is different but still delicious.

Oysters three ways

SERVES 2 AS A STARTER

FRESH OYSTERS WITH A BEER
VINAIGRETTE DRESSING
250 ml (9 fl oz/1 cup) Belgian fruit beer,
    such as Kriek or Framboise
2 teaspoons sugar
3 tablespoons vegetable oil
1 tablespoon snipped chives
1½ teaspoons finger lime pulp ('roe')
    (see note)
6 oysters, on the shell

STOUT-BATTERED OYSTERS
3 tablespoons plain (all-purpose) flour
330 ml (11¼ fl oz) Coopers Best
    Extra Stout
6 oysters, on the shell
vegetable or peanut oil, for deep-frying

SALT AND PEPPER OYSTERS WITH
A MEDITERRANEAN SALSA
1 tablespoon very finely diced red onion
1 tablespoon very finely chopped
    kalamata olives
1 tablespoon finely chopped tomato flesh
    (peel the tomato, remove the seeds
    and reserve some juice)
3 tablespoons rice flour
6 oysters, on the shell
vegetable or peanut oil, for shallow-frying

If you can't find finger limes,
use finely diced lime flesh. Finger
limes are seasonally available from
select greengrocers.

Fresh oysters with a beer vinaigrette dressing

Put the beer and sugar in a small saucepan over gentle heat and reduce down to about 3 tablespoons. Pour into a bowl and, when cooled, whisk in the vegetable oil. Season with salt and freshly ground black pepper and add the snipped chives. Spoon some of the beer vinaigrette over a fresh oyster and top with about ¼ teaspoon of finger lime pulp.

Stout-battered oysters

The secret of getting a really good crispy batter is to have the batter as cold as possible — make it in a bowl that is sitting over another bowl filled with ice. Put the flour into the top bowl with a pinch of salt (and any other herbs or spices you want) and then pour in some of the stout. Stir the batter but don't overwork it. Make the batter as thick or thin as you prefer — for this dish it should be a thinner batter than you would use for beer-battered fish.

Fill a deep-fryer, wok or heavy-based saucepan one-third with oil and heat to 180°C (350°F), or until a cube of bread dropped into the oil browns in 15 seconds. Remove the oysters from their shells and dip them into the batter. Let the excess drain off for about half a second and then fry batches of the oysters until golden and crisp. Remove with a slotted spoon and drain on crumpled paper towel. Put the oysters back onto their shells for serving.

Salt and pepper oysters with a Mediterranean salsa

Mix together the onion, olives and tomato to make a salsa.

Place the rice flour and a generous pinch of salt and pepper in a bowl and give it all a mix.

Remove the oysters from their shells and coat them in the flour, dusting off any excess. Fry the oysters in vegetable or peanut oil until coloured and crisp. Drain on some paper towel and then put the oysters back onto their shell for serving.

Place a teaspoon of the salsa on top of each oyster. Spoon a little of the reserved tomato liquid over the salsa.

Here is a really simple but delicious salad that will accompany anything from fresh crab to a succulent steak.

Mixed leaf salad with speck

SERVES 2-4 AS A SIDE (DEPENDING HOW HUNGRY YOU ARE)

Put the lettuce, mustard cress, pine nuts and speck in a bowl and then drizzle in the olive oil and balsamic. Season with salt and pepper and serve. See what I mean about simple?

3 handfuls (about 185 g/6½ oz) of
    freshly picked mixed lettuce leaves
1 handful red mustard cress (see note)
3 tablespoons pine nuts, lightly toasted
80 g (2¾ oz) fried, chopped speck or
    bacon lardons
3 tablespoons extra virgin olive oil
3 tablespoons balsamic vinegar

Red mustard cress has a lovely spicy and slightly hot flavour similar to mustard.

Snail and yabby leek pie

MAKES 4-6

about 36 fresh, farmed snails to get
    1 cup of snail meat
about 12 raw yabbies (or langoustines
    or large prawns/shrimp)
olive oil
4 thyme sprigs
¼ teaspoon ground cumin
1 leek, quartered and thinly sliced
1 garlic clove, crushed
2 celery stalks, diced
2 carrots, diced
3 potatoes, diced
30 g (1 oz) butter
3 tablespoons plain (all-purpose) flour
250 ml (9 fl oz/1 cup) hot chicken stock
250 ml (9 fl oz/1 cup) Hunter Kolsch
10 saffron threads, soaked in
    1–2 tablespoons water
1 teaspoon curry powder
155 g (5½ oz/¾ cup) peas
6 sourdough buns (see note)
sesame seeds, for sprinkling

If you don't have sourdough buns, you can use ramekins and top them with a puff pastry lid and press to seal. Brush the top of the pie with beaten egg and cut a cross in the lid so that steam can escape. Sprinkle with sesame seeds and bake until the puff pastry is golden brown and crisp.

Even though the snails will have been purged, it is best to boil them twice to make sure they are good and clean and to get rid of any excess mucus. Fill a large saucepan with water, add a large pinch of salt and then throw in your snails. Bring the water to the boil and boil for 10 minutes. Drain, then repeat the process. Drain again and set the snails aside until they are cool enough to touch. Use a toothpick to carefully pick the snail meat out of the shells and put it in a bowl.

Meanwhile, boil the yabbies in a separate saucepan of salted water for about 2 minutes. Remove the shells, collect the tail meat and chop it — you should have about 1 cup of chopped meat.

Preheat the oven to 230°C (450°F/Gas 8). Add a splash of olive oil to a frying pan, then gently cook the snail and yabby meat for 2–3 minutes, with the thyme, cumin, and some salt and pepper. Remove from the pan and keep warm. Add a little more oil and fry off the leek for a couple of minutes, then add the garlic and fry gently for a few minutes more. Add the celery, carrot and potato and cook for a few minutes, stirring so it doesn't stick to the bottom of the pan.

Meanwhile, melt the butter in a saucepan and, when it is foaming, gradually stir in the flour to make a roux, making sure to mix the flour and butter well. Cook gently, stirring for several minutes to cook out the flour taste, then slowly add the hot chicken stock and beer, mixing until you have a smooth, thick stock or sauce. Season with the saffron, curry powder, and some salt and pepper.

Add the sauce to the vegetables and simmer until the vegetables are cooked to your liking, stirring every now and then. Add the peas, and snail and yabby meat, including any juices from the meat. Allow it to come back to a gentle simmer.

Hollow out the sourdough buns and bake them in the oven until dry and crisp. Spoon the snail and yabby mixture into the buns, then sprinkle with sesame seeds and serve.

Crouton of quail on wild mushroom pâté with asparagus and quail glaze

RECIPE BY IAN MORPHY FROM THE OLD GEORGE AND DRAGON, EAST MAITLAND

SERVES 6

For the croutons: Preheat the oven to 180°C (350°F/Gas 4). Butter the slices of bread with butter, then lay out on a baking tray and bake for 10 minutes until crisp, turning once, then set aside. Increase the oven temperature to 200°C (400°F/Gas 6).

For the pâté: Sweat the onion in 50 g (1¾ oz) of the butter in a frying pan over medium heat, then add the field mushrooms and cook until coloured, then tip into a large saucepan. Melt another 50 g (1¾ oz) butter and cook the Swiss browns until coloured and the liquid has evaporated, then add to the saucepan. Finally, cook the frozen porcini in the remaining butter. Cook until they are brown and all the liquid has evaporated, then add to the saucepan together with herbs and cream. Bring to the boil and boil until reduced by about half. Stir in the arrowroot. Blend coarsely and set aside.

For the quail: Loosely drape 2 bacon slices over each quail breast. Stuff each bird with a sprig of thyme. Roast for about 12 minutes for large birds, less for smaller birds. The idea is to keep the breast pink — rest for 5 minutes, then remove the breasts from the carcass.

For the sauce: Chop the quail carcasses and legs and put in a saucepan on medium–high heat. Cover with chicken stock and add the white wine. Reduce to a thin sauce consistency, strain and swirl in the butter.

To assemble, reheat the quail breast briefly in the oven, put 2 croutons on each plate and pile on some warm mushroom pâté. Remove the quail skin and slice the breasts to fan over the pâté. Finish with a drizzle of sauce and some asparagus.

CROUTONS
1 sourdough baguette, sliced into pieces 1 cm (½ inch) thick
butter, for brushing

PÂTÉ
½ onion, finely chopped
150 g (5½ oz) butter
300 g (10½ oz) field mushrooms, chopped
300 g (10½ oz) Swiss brown mushrooms, roughly chopped
400 g (14 oz) frozen porcini mushrooms, defrosted and sliced
2 tablespoons chopped parsley
2 tablespoons chopped tarragon
150 g (5½ oz) thick (double/heavy) cream
1 tablespoon arrowroot in 60 ml (2 fl oz/¼ cup) water

QUAIL
6 large quail – approx 300 g (10½ oz) each
12 bacon slices
6 thyme sprigs

SAUCE
quail carcasses, legs reserved
500 ml (17 fl oz/2 cups) chicken stock
100 ml (3½ fl oz) dry white wine
50 g (1¾ oz) butter

Tandoori goat burgers

SERVES 4

1 onion, finely diced

1 garlic clove, finely chopped

1 egg

1 tablespoon finely chopped rosemary

4 tablespoons ready-made tandoori paste

650 g (1 lb 7 oz) minced (ground) goat
(make sure it is not too lean or the
meat will be dry — see note)

1 red capsicum (pepper)

olive oil

1 garlic clove, extra, crushed

1 eggplant (aubergine)

4 sourdough buns

200–250 g (7–9 oz) block of feta cheese
in brine, drained and thinly sliced

1 large handful rocket (arugula)

Using your hands, mix the onion, chopped garlic, egg, rosemary and tandoori paste through the goat meat until it is very well incorporated, then season with salt and pepper and mix again. (It may be a good idea to use gloves to avoid staining your hands with the tandoori paste.) Cover and let it stand while you prepare the vegetables.

To prepare the capsicum, slice the sides from the core and place them, skin side up, under a hot grill (broiler). Let them blister and burn until blackened and then place them in a plastic bag to sweat for 5 minutes. Peel the skins off and place the flesh into a bowl. Pour over some olive oil and crushed garlic.

To prepare the eggplant, slice thin pieces lengthways down the eggplant, then brush with olive oil (which, if you like, could have crushed garlic in it) and grill (broil) or fry on one side until browned, then brush the uncooked side with oil and turn and cook until browned. Allow to drain on some paper towel.

Divide the goat mixture and form four patties. Heat some oil in a frying pan or on the barbecue grill and fry the patties until cooked through.

Cut the buns in half and toast. Place a tandoori patty on each bun and top with a slice of capsicum, a slice of eggplant, a few thin slices of feta and, lastly, some rocket. Put the top on the bun and serve with a good hoppy beer like Little Creatures Pale Ale or a Matilda Bay Alpha Ale.

Goat meat is available from gourmet butchers but this recipe will work just as well with lamb.
If you prefer, you can buy pre-marinated capsicum and eggplant.

Goose egg pasta with roasted pumpkin, garlic and butter sauce

SERVES 4

Preheat the oven to 200°C (400°F/Gas 6). Roast the pumpkin and garlic in the oven for 15–20 minutes, or until tender — don't overcook the pumpkin as you don't want it to fall apart in the sauce. Set aside and leave the garlic in the skin.

For the pasta dough: Combine the two flours together and season with salt. Pile the flour on a bench and then make a well in the centre. Crack 1 goose egg into the well and mix. Once it's combined do the same with the next egg and then again with the last egg. If the mixture is wet, sprinkle with a little more flour. Knead well for 10 minutes and then cover with plastic wrap and let it rest for 10–15 minutes.

Cut the pasta dough into three pieces, then flatten out each piece. Using one piece at a time, put it through your pasta-making machine, following the manufacturer's instructions. Run it through the widest setting, then fold the dough in half lengthways; repeat four times. Reduce the settings on the pasta machine, feeding and rolling the pasta through each setting four times until the dough is translucent and very thin. Cut the long flat pasta in half lengthways and then feed it through your chosen cutter setting. Sprinkle flour over the pasta and give it a toss through to prevent the pasta from sticking together. Repeat with the remaining dough.

For the sauce: In a frying pan over medium heat, melt the butter, then grate in the nutmeg, when the butter begins to foam, add the roasted pumpkin. Squeeze the garlic out of the skins, breaking it up between your fingers, and sprinkle it around the pan, then throw in the pine nuts, tear some basil leaves roughly and toss everything together.

Put your pasta in a large saucepan of well-salted boiling water and give it a gentle mix so that it is not sticking together. Cook for 2–3 minutes.

When the pasta is cooked, use tongs to lift it out of the water and put it into the pan with the pumpkin sauce. Give it all a really good mix, and serve with the remaining basil and parmesan.

150 g (5½ oz) butternut pumpkin (squash), cut into 2 cm (¾ inch) cubes
10 garlic cloves, unpeeled
125 g (4½ oz) butter
½ fresh nutmeg
80 g (2¾ oz/½ cup) pine nuts, toasted in a dry frying pan
1 handful basil
grated parmesan, to serve

PASTA
125 g (4½ oz/1 cup) '00' flour (see note)
125 g (4½ oz/1 cup) semolina
3 goose eggs

'00' flour is a highly refined wheat flour with a low protein content, ideal for smooth pasta dough. It is available from delicatessens.

The great thing about this beer is that it works so wonderfully with the delicate nature and sweetness of the spatchcock. The Franziskaner Hefe Weissbier is a lovely rich, cloudy wheat beer with notes of banana, clove and other fruity and sour overtones. The salty sweetness of the prosciutto complements the banana and clove character in the beer, the sourness of the wheat enhances the delicate flavour of the bird and the prunes and apricot lift it all up. In my opinion, wheat beers are great beers to cook with. If you can't get Franziskaner you could use Schöfferhofer, Erdinger, Hoegaarden or a local wheat beer.

Beer-braised spatchcock   SERVES 6

6 x 500 g (1 lb 2 oz) spatchcocks
(poussins) for one per person or
3 x 800 g (1 lb 12 oz) spatchcocks
for half per person
24 dried prunes
24 dried apricots
12 prosciutto slices
olive oil
2 x 500 ml (17 fl oz) bottles
Franziskaner Hefe Weissbier (see note)

Preheat the oven to 180°C (350°F/Gas 4). Wash and dry the spatchcocks. Place the prunes and apricots into the cavities of the birds and tie the legs together, then wrap the prosciutto around the birds and secure with toothpicks. If you are using the bigger birds then put 8 prunes and 8 apricots in each bird and wrap each bird in 4 slices of the prosciutto. Brown each bird on all sides in a hot frying pan with olive oil then place in a roasting tin.

Pour in the beer so that it comes about halfway up the side of the birds. Cover the tray with foil, tightly sealing the sides — use two pieces of foil to form a tent over the top of the tray. Once tightly sealed, pierce the foil once so the steam can escape then place in the oven. Cook for 1½–2 hours, or until the juices run clear when pierced with a skewer.

Remove the spatchcocks from the pan and keep warm. Pour the pan juices through a sieve and into a small clean saucepan, bring to the boil and then reduce the heat to a simmer and reduce the juice down to about a third and until it has a nice shiny consistency.

Place a whole or half spatchcock on a plate, depending on how you are serving it, and drizzle some of the sauce around and over it. Serve with a green salad and a side of rice or a medley of seasonal steamed vegetables.

There are two Franziskaner Hefe Weissbiere — a pale or 'hell' and a dark or 'dunkel'. For this recipe use the pale as it complements the spatchcock. If you can't get Franziskaner, try a locally made German-style wheat beer.

Laksa johore

RECIPE BY CAROL SELVA RAJAH, AUTHOR OF *HEAVENLY FRAGRANCE*

SERVES 4

Grind the lemongrass, galangal and ginger using a mortar and pestle or small food processor.

Place the prawn shells, fish bones and water in a wok and gently simmer for 10 minutes to make a stock. Strain and return to the wok, discarding the shells and bones. Simmer the prawns and fish cubes in the stock for 3–5 minutes or until soft. Strain again, once again reserving the stock. Place the prawns and fish in a food processor and blend until smooth.

Heat the oil in a wok and fry the shrimp paste and ground lemongrass mixture over high heat until aromatic. Add the blended fish and prawns and stir until it sticks to the pan.

Add the curry powder, chilli powder and tamarind purée with 500 ml (17 fl oz/2 cups) of the reserved stock. Add the coconut milk and toasted coconut and simmer until cooked, about 10–12 minutes. Add the lime juice and some salt and pepper. Stir in the coconut cream, then remove from the heat without allowing to boil.

To serve, blanch the noodles in boiling water, strain and arrange in bowls. Top with the soup and arrange the garnishes on a platter on the side.

2 lemongrass stems, white part only, chopped
3 cm (1¼ inch) piece fresh galangal, chopped
2 cm (¾ inch) piece fresh ginger, chopped
300 g (10½ oz) prawns (shrimp), peeled, reserving the shells for stock
500 g (1 lb 2 oz) ling, cubed, reserving the bones for stock
1 litre (35 fl oz/4 cups) water
1 tablespoon oil
1 teaspoon shrimp paste, dry-roasted in foil (optional)
2 tablespoons fish curry powder
1 tablespoon chilli powder, or to taste
1 tablespoon tamarind purée
400 ml (14 fl oz) tin coconut milk
3 tablespoons desiccated coconut, toasted
juice of 1 lime
125 ml (4 fl oz/½ cup) coconut cream
200 g (7 oz) dried rice noodles

GARNISH
2 limes, quartered
1 Lebanese (short) cucumber, shredded
2 large handfuls of Vietnamese mint
50 g (1¾ oz/½ cup) bean sprouts, trimmed
2 red onions, thinly sliced
2 tablespoons chilli sauce (to taste)
ready-made fried onions

Stuffed sweet capsicums

SERVES 6 AS A STARTER OR 3 AS A MAIN

95 g (3¼ oz/½ cup) wild rice
100 g (3½ oz/½ cup) basmati rice
1 chorizo sausage, diced
olive oil
2 garlic cloves, finely chopped
400 g (14 oz) minced (ground) turkey
2 teaspoons chopped coriander
　　(cilantro) leaves
2 tomatoes, peeled, seeded and chopped
¼–½ red onion, finely diced
1 avocado, diced
6 sweet red capsicums (peppers)
oil spray

SAUCE
400 g (14 oz) tin of chopped tomatoes
1 teaspoon smoky tomatina spice mix
　　(see page 128)
¼ teaspoon chilli powder
20 g (¾ oz) grated 70% cocoa
　　dark chocolate
blueberries, to serve
1 handful of coriander (cilantro) leaves,
　　to serve

Cook the wild rice in a large saucepan of boiling water for about 1 hour, or until the rice cracks and splits open. Meanwhile, cook the basmati rice in boiling water until tender, drain.

Preheat the oven to 180°C (350°F/Gas 4). In a frying pan, fry the chorizo in a splash of olive oil until it starts to colour, then add the garlic and cook for a few minutes before adding the turkey, giving it a good stir to break the meat up. Once the turkey is just cooked through, season with salt and pepper and mix in the coriander, then remove from the pan and set aside.

Mix the two rices, tomato, onion and avocado together, then add the meat and thoroughly mix. Cut the capsicums on the diagonal about 3–4 cm (1¼–1½ inches) from the stem, remove the seeds and then stuff with the rice and meat mix, using the thick end of a chopstick to push the stuffing deep down into the bottom of the capsicum. Stuff the lid also.

Lay the stuffed capsicum on a lightly oiled baking tray and place the lid of each capsicum against the one it was cut from. The capsicum will almost look whole again. Spray with a little olive oil and cook for about 20–30 minutes until the capsicums are softened and coloured.

For the sauce: Blitz the tomatoes into a purée in a blender, then bring to a simmer in a saucepan. Add the tomatina and chilli and simmer for a few minutes, then add the grated chocolate and make sure it melts completely through the sauce. Check for seasoning.

To serve, put some sauce in the middle of a plate and place a capsicum and its lid on top of the sauce. Scatter some blueberries around the capsicum and in the sauce, then garnish with some coriander.

Eggplant with haloumi and fried tortillas

BY NADINE ABENSUR, AUTHOR OF *NADINE'S VEGETARIAN COOKBOOK*

SERVES 6 AS A STARTER

Make up a dressing with 4 tablespoons of the olive oil, the lemon juice, garlic, Tabasco and some salt.

Place the eggplants on the barbecue (otherwise use the naked flame on the stove) and cook, turning regularly, for about 8 minutes until they are charred and the skin comes away easily. Prick with a fork to test they are soft all the way through.

Meanwhile, to make the chickpea and broad bean salad, cook the broad beans in a large saucepan of boiling water for 7 minutes, then drain and refresh under cold water. Drain again and slip the grey skin off each bean. Mix everything together except the herbs and leave to marinate for 20 minutes. Taste and adjust the spicing if necessary. Mix in most of the herbs at the last minute, reserving a little to scatter on top.

Pop the eggplants on a board and make cuts in them approximately 1 cm (½ inch) apart, without cutting all the way through. Remove the charred skin by inserting the point of a fine blade under it and lifting it off. Place the eggplants on a serving plate and douse generously with the dressing and the herbs.

For the haloumi, brush the cheese slices with olive oil and Tabasco, place on a chargrill pan until nicely cooked on both sides.

Heat the remaining oil in a frying pan and fry the tortillas one at a time, until golden on both sides, puffy and patched with black.

Serve the tortillas with the eggplant, haloumi and the chickpea salad.

125 ml (4 fl oz/½ cup) olive oil
juice of 1 lemon
2 garlic cloves, chopped
dash of Tabasco sauce
4 large eggplants (aubergines)
basil and coriander (cilantro) leaves,
    for garnish
6 flour tortillas

CHICKPEA SALAD
500 g (1 lb 2 oz) frozen broad (fava) beans
400 g (14 oz) tin of chickpeas, rinsed
    and drained
1 small red onion, finely diced
2 garlic cloves, chopped
1 tablespoon ground cumin
1 tablespoon paprika
100 ml (3½ fl oz) olive oil
1 tablespoon tamari
juice of ½ lemon
dash of Tabasco sauce
chopped coriander leaves
chopped flat-leaf (Italian) parsley

HALOUMI
250 g (9 oz) haloumi cheese, sliced
olive oil, for brushing
dash of Tabasco sauce

The quality of the pork is the key to this recipe. We have used Bangalow sweet pork from the Byron Bay hinterland. The loin should be tied by the butcher and the rind scored. If you are using a bone-in roast, it is not necessary to tie it.

Bangalow sweet pork roast with anchovy sauce

RECIPE BY DAUD KENDALL FROM BYRON BAY BEACH CAFÉ

SERVES 6

1.5 kg (3 lb 5 oz) pork loin, rind on
1 tablespoon oil
125 ml (4 fl oz/½ cup) water

SAUCE
3 tablespoons extra virgin olive oil
4 garlic cloves, crushed
2 anchovy fillets, crushed
2 teaspoons chopped rosemary
2 tablespoons balsamic vinegar

Preheat the oven to 200°C (400°F/Gas 6). Dry the pork well with paper towels. Rub the rind surface lightly with oil and rub in a generous amount of sea salt. Sit the pork on a rack in a roasting tin and place into the oven for 30 minutes. Reduce the heat to 180°C (350°F/Gas 4) and pour the water into the base of the tin to prevent the fat from splattering.

Cook for a further 1 hour, then turn on the top element or place under a preheated grill (broiler) for about 5–10 minutes to make the crackling nice and crisp. Set the pork on a plate and rest in a warm place for at least 15 minutes.

For the anchovy sauce: Heat the olive oil in a frying pan over medium heat, add the garlic and fry until lightly golden, then add the anchovies and rosemary and fry for 30 seconds. Splash in the balsamic vinegar and remove the pan from the heat.

Serve the pork with the anchovy sauce and roasted vegetables.

Indian-style fried snapper

SERVES 4

Use a mortar and pestle to bash the onion, garlic, lemongrass, turmeric, chilli and a generous pinch of salt into a paste. Take the whole fish and make a few deep slits in the flesh on each side. Season the fish with salt and then rub the paste all over the fish and especially deep into the cuts. Leave to marinate for an hour or two.

Heat the oil in a frying pan large enough to hold the fish. Season the oil with the cumin seeds, mustard seeds and chilli, allowing them to fry for a minute or so, then lay the fish in the pan. Fry on one side until golden and the flesh flakes when tested with a fork, then turn the fish over and fry until golden and cooked.

Serve with a fresh garden salad.

1 onion, chopped
4 garlic cloves, roughly chopped
2 lemongrass stems, chopped
1 teaspoon ground chopped turmeric
2 teaspoons chopped chilli
1 whole plate size snapper, scaled and gutted (get the biggest snapper you can that will fit into your largest frying pan)
vegetable or peanut oil, for pan-frying
1 teaspoon cumin seeds
1 teaspoon black mustard seeds
1 green chilli, thinly sliced

When choosing a whole fish make sure the eyes are bright and clear. Don't be frightened to smell the fish, it should smell of clean, fresh ocean — if it smells 'fishy' — don't buy it.

This recipe came about after I visited a garlic farm just outside of Byron Bay. Garlic farmers extraordinaire, Daryl and Kerry, grow a variety of large Russian garlic. Each bulb is about twice the size of my thumb. Russian garlic is delicious eaten raw and just as delicious roasted and smashed into avocado.

Byron guacamole

SERVES 4 AS A STARTER

4 fresh jalapeño peppers
8 large garlic cloves, unpeeled
1 teaspoon olive oil
2 avocados, diced
juice of ½ lemon
corn chips, to serve

Preheat the oven to 180°C (350°F/Gas 4). Char the jalapeños over a naked flame until the skin is blackened and blistered and then put them into a plastic bag to sweat for about 5 minutes — this will make them easier to peel. Lay the garlic on a sheet of foil, drizzle with the olive oil, then wrap tightly and put in the oven for about 15 minutes, or until the cloves are lovely and soft.

Peel and seed the jalapeños, then chop the flesh. Squeeze the roasted garlic cloves out of their skins and place in a bowl with the jalapeños. Mix through the diced avocado, then dress with lemon juice and season with salt and pepper.

Serve the guacamole with corn chips.

If you can't get the Russian garlic then keep an eye out for Mexican garlic as they can also be quite large. Put in as little or as much as you like! The same goes for the jalapeños — adjust the amount to suit your own heat threshold.

Mediterranean rack of goat with spring vegetables

RECIPE BY ROBERT MOLINES FROM BISTRO MOLINES, HUNTER VALLEY

SERVES 2

Preheat the oven to 190°C (375°F/Gas 5). Heat a splash of olive oil in a frying pan, then sear the racks of goat. Transfer to a roasting tin, sprinkle with the thyme, rosemary and garlic and cook the goat for about 20 minutes.

Heat a splash of olive oil in another frying pan and sauté the spring vegetables together. Season with salt and pepper and continue to cook until the vegetables are tender.

When the goat is cooked, remove from the pan to rest. Leave the herbs and garlic in the pan along with the juices. Place the pan over medium heat and deglaze with the white wine and simmer until reduced by two-thirds.

Plate each rack of goat on a serving plate, arrange the vegetables next to it and spoon the sauce over the top. Voila!

olive oil

2 x lean goat racks, 8 points
    each, trimmed

4 thyme sprigs

4 rosemary sprigs

3 garlic cloves, sliced

½ radicchio heart, cut in half lengthways

2 baby zucchini (courgettes)

2 baby carrots

8 baby artichokes

6 cherry tomatoes

125 ml (4 fl oz/½ cup) dry white wine

Goats have been the mainstay of some Mediterranean communities for centuries. They provide milk which is used for cheese and yoghurt and, of course, they are great eating.

Baklava

MAKES 24 PIECES

2 x 375 g (13 oz) packet of filo pastry
200 g (7 oz) unsalted butter, melted

SYRUP
350 g (12 oz/1 cup) honey
170 g (5¾ oz/¾ cup) caster
   (superfine) sugar
100 ml (3½ fl oz) orange juice
1 cinnamon stick
3 strips of orange zest
250 ml (9 fl oz/1 cup) water

FILLING
150 g (5½ oz/1½ cups) walnuts
150 g (5½ oz/1 cup) pistachio nuts
150 g (5½ oz) macadamia nuts
grated zest of 1 lemon
½ teaspoon ground cardamom
3 tablespoons caster (superfine) sugar
2 teaspoons rosewater

For the syrup: Place all the ingredients in a saucepan over low heat, stirring to dissolve the sugar. Increase the heat and bring to the boil. Once boiled do not stir any more. Simmer gently for 15 minutes or until syrupy.

For the filling: Put all the ingredients in a blender and pulse until well combined and the nuts are finely chopped.

Preheat the oven to 180°C (350°F/Gas 4). Depending on the size of your baking tin — a 20 x 30 cm (8 x 12 inch) tin is ideal — you may need to cut the filo pastry to size before starting the layering process so that each sheet fits snugly into the tin. You'll need 36 sheets of filo to fit into a rectangular cake tin. Brush the base of the tin with the melted butter and then lay down one sheet of filo pastry. Brush this sheet with the melted butter then lay down another sheet and brush this with butter. Continue doing this until you have laid down 12 sheets. Now spread half of the nut filling evenly over the filo. Take a sheet of filo and place it over the filling and then brush this with butter, then lay another sheet down and brush this with butter, continue to do this until you have another 12 layers down and then spread the remaining nut mixture over the top of this. Finally lay and butter another 12 sheets of filo but do not butter the very last one.

Cut the baklava diagonally across the pan from left to right every 5 cm (2 inches) and then again from right to left so as to create a diamond pattern — don't cut all the way through to the base as you want the honey syrup to sit in the baklava and not just on the bottom of it. Put into the oven, spray the top with some water so that it doesn't burn and cook for 40–50 minutes or until nicely browned and crisp on the top.

Remove from the oven and immediately pour the syrup all over the baklava and listen to it sizzle. Allow to cool overnight and then cut through the bottom and serve.

Keep the sheets of filo pastry covered with a damp cloth while you work so that it doesn't dry out, or else the sheets will stick together and tear.

Flaming oranges

SERVES 4-6

200 g (7 oz) raw (demerara) sugar
200 ml (7 fl oz) water
pinch of ground cardamom
½ teaspoon ground cinnamon
1 cinnamon stick
2 cloves
2 tablespoons thinly sliced mint,
    plus some whole leaves
6 oranges, peeled and segmented
125 ml (4 fl oz/½ cup) Grand Marnier
vanilla ice cream, to serve

Make a sugar syrup by combining the sugar and water and heating over medium heat until the sugar has melted, then bring to a simmer and cook for several minutes. Turn off the heat and allow the syrup to cool. Once cool, add the spices and sliced mint and whisk to combine then add the orange pieces and mix again. Allow the oranges to marinate for a couple of hours.

Put the oranges and syrup into a heatproof serving bowl, making sure to stack the oranges so they climb up out of the syrup like a pyramid. Pour the Grand Marnier into a metal ladle or a small saucepan and hold over a flame, gently heating the liqueur. It will eventually light and begin to burn especially if you tilt the ladle or pan so that the liquid is close the flame — when this happens turn all the lights out in the room and then pour over the oranges and watch as they 'flame'. If you don't have gas, warm the Grand Marnier in a small saucepan over low heat. Tilt the saucepan away from you and hold a long-handled lighter near the pan and click to start a flame — it will then flame in the same way.

When it stops burning turn the lights on and serve the oranges in individual bowls with some of the lovely syrup now infused with the Grand Marnier. Garnish with a mint leaf and a side serve of vanilla ice cream.

Green tea and Buddha's hand ice cream

Heat 125 ml (4 fl oz/½ cup) of the milk in a saucepan until quite warm but not boiling. Add the green tea and let it steep for a minute or 2 still over the heat. The tea will soak up most of the milk so pour in the remaining milk after the tea has steeped for the first minute. Pour the milk and tea through a fine sieve into a clean saucepan. Squash the tea leaves with the back of a spoon to extract as much of the milk as possible. Discard the leaves. At this point the milk will taste very bitter but don't worry.

Using a vegetable peeler, peel thin strips of the green skin off the Buddha's hand — all the fragrance and flavour comes from the skin. Add the strips of skin to the milk along with the cream, egg and sugar. Heat the milk over medium heat and stir until the sugar has dissolved. Allow the skin to steep in the milk for at least 10 minutes.

Remove the pan from the heat and remove the skin peelings. Transfer the mixture to a shallow bowl and place in the freezer to chill. Once cold enough, put it in your ice-cream machine and churn until you arrive at the desired consistency. Depending on your machine this could take between 30 minutes and 1 hour.

Put the ice cream in a bowl or container and leave in the freezer until you are ready to serve. Keep in mind that ice cream made like this will melt very quickly so it is often better to serve in a martini type glass with a little fruit on the top as a garnish if you wish. If you leave the ice cream in the freezer for a couple of days it will become harder.

250 ml (9 fl oz/1 cup) milk
10 teaspoons green leaf tea
1 Buddha's hand (use a green one as it is more intense than one that has gone yellow — see note)
500 ml (17 fl oz/2 cups) cream
1 egg, beaten
165 g (5¾ oz/¾ cup) sugar

Buddha's hand is an unusual variety of citrus fruit. The fruit resembles a hand with finger-like segments. The peel is used to flavour desserts, salads and seafood. If you can't find a Buddha's hand, you can use the zest from 1 lime and 1 lemon as a substitute.

Avocado panna cotta with raspberry coulis

SERVES 8

250 ml (9 fl oz/1 cup) milk

1 large avocado, flesh removed, chopped

750 ml (26 fl oz/3 cups) cream

125 g (4½ oz) caster (superfine) sugar

½ vanilla bean

4 titanium gelatine sheets
(total 20 g/¾ oz) or 1½ tablespoons
powdered gelatine

COULIS

150 g of raspberries (fresh or frozen)

3 tablespoons raw (demerara) sugar

3 tablespoons caster (superfine) sugar

3 tablespoons water

Put the milk and avocado in a blender and purée until well combined and smooth. Put the cream and caster sugar in a saucepan, then split the vanilla bean and scrape out the seeds with the tip of a knife and add them and the bean itself to the cream. Slowly bring to the boil. Remove from the heat and add the milk and avocado mixture and gently combine — you do not want to create air bubbles on the surface.

Put the gelatine leaves into cold water and soak for about 7 minutes, then squeeze out the water and add the leaves to the hot cream mixture. Carefully fold through until they are all dissolved.

If you are using powdered gelatine, use 3 tablespoons of the milk and sprinkle the gelatine over it, leave for a few minutes, then stir into the hot cream mix. Pour into eight 125 ml (4 fl oz/½ cup) glasses and put in the fridge for 3 hours or until well set.

For the coulis: Put the raspberries in a saucepan with the sugars and water and bring to the boil, then simmer for 7-10 minutes until you get the consistency you desire. I like to mash the fruit with a fork as it cooks down so that it is pulpy. Set aside to cool. Then blend and strain the mixture.

Streak some coulis across each plate then dip the panna cotta moulds into hot water to warm up the panna cotta so it will slip easily out of the mould and place it on the sauce. Place a little more sauce on top of the panna cotta. If serving in a glass just place a teaspoon or so of the sauce in the middle of the panna cotta.

QUEENSLAND

You can go surfing in the morning and again in the afternoon, dine out in a range of little restaurants and on the weekends, cruise around the food markets held in many of the small towns dotted around the state. Yep, sounds good to me.

The land of sun and surf, the place where Aussies like to go when they retire and, if you ask me, that is not such a bad idea. Why not move to a place where it is warm most of the year and fairly hot the rest of the time?

Queensland is a state of opposites: you have your tourist holiday destinations such as the Gold Coast and in contrast, the hinterland where you will find some wonderful and sometimes slightly crazy people. I'm talking about Alla and Michael Ward from Mount Tamborine Distillery — Alla is the distiller (a lovely quiet and dedicated producer) and Michael is probably the maddest person I have ever had the pleasure of having on the show! I am not sure how much of what we shot when we visited made it on to the show, as neither of us really made much sense, but we certainly had a ball shooting there. Oh, and it was not the wonderful spirits that they make that caused the silliness — Michael doesn't drink! Check out the gado gado recipe and order some of his banana liqueur before you make it. Then there was Katrina who specialises in growing chillies. She conducted a chilli-tasting session with me and mistakenly gave me one of the hottest chillies first, believing it was the mildest, so of course I ate the whole thing and very quickly lost the ability to talk.

Further up you have the Sunshine Coast which is a little more laid-back yet a bit more sophisticated. I cooked emu rice-paper rolls at the fabulous Spirit House Restaurant in Yandina, spanner crab and squid-ink pasta at the famous Berardo's Restaurant in Noosa, and went for an early morning surf with the world champion long-board rider, Josh Constable. In Queensland, it's all about good food and lifestyle and these are two of the reasons I never tire of touring around this great state.

Travelling further north, you get to Townsville, where I shot two episodes. I cooked up some beautiful farmed banana prawns for Robbie, the opera-singing sugar cane farmer and his extended family — all fifty of them! It must be Queensland's famous hospitality that saw me do another cook-up for the good folk at Wambiana Station. Michael, the station owner, put me to work doing some cattle rustling and then his wife Michelle put me to work cooking up beef ribs and beer damper for the family — again all fifty of them! The recipe is in the following pages but it is only for two so give it a go.

Finally we got to Cairns, which is a really great place but flaming hot in summer, which, of course, was when we visited. I had my first taste of crocodile and one had its first taste of me; thankfully though it was only a few weeks old but by golly they have sharp teeth! I cooked my veal roulades for veal farmers Bruce and Elizabeth which they politely claimed to love and I went pineapple picking for a very exhausting and sweaty hour — those guys work hard!

These are perfect for finger-food as you can hold them and eat them with one hand while you hold your beer or chardonnay in the other. The prawns are sweet, nutty and meaty while the asparagus is still slightly crisp and also sweet — delicious!

Beer-marinated prawns with crisp asparagus spears
SERVES 4 AS A STARTER

1 kg (2 lb 4 oz) large prawns (shrimp), peeled and deveined, leaving the tails intact

5 large garlic cloves, mashed with 1 teaspoon of salt

fresh asparagus spears, trimmed, 2 per prawn

MARINADE

3 tablespoons olive oil

170 ml (5½ fl oz/⅔ cup) beer (a good hoppy pale ale)

3 tablespoons lime juice

3 spring onions (scallions), finely chopped

2 teaspoons coriander seeds, toasted then crushed

2 teaspoons cumin seeds, toasted then crushed

1 handful of coriander (cilantro) leaves,

1 red chilli, thinly sliced

soy sauce, to taste

Rub the prawns with the garlic and salt mixture and let stand, covered, for 1–2 hours.

For the marinade: Combine the marinade ingredients in a bowl and mix well. Add the prawns to the marinade, coat thoroughly and marinate in the fridge for several hours.

Spear the prawns with a knife so as to make a hole between the tail end and the head end, taking care not to slice open the prawn. Weave the spears of asparagus through the first hole and then continue to thread the asparagus through the hole. Return the now-skewered prawn to the marinade until all the prawns are likewise skewered and ready to be cooked.

Chargrill the prawns on the barbecue — put some olive oil on a preheated hotplate and throw all the prawns on the barbie. Cook until coloured and crispy on one side and then turn and cook the other side. When cooked pile them up on a plate and hand them out.

I love marinating in beer as it adds great flavour as well as helping to tenderise meat. There are two rules — don't use light beer and only use beer you love to drink.

These are lovely rich, succulent ribs when cooked long and slow so make sure you give them the time to cook — they should be melting off the bone. Also don't do what I did when I cooked these for about 50 people — if you fill your oven up with three trays of ribs, they are going to take a lot longer to cook than just eight ribs. I had a lot of hungry people patiently waiting for dinner and a TV producer who was getting a little cranky!

Beef ribs in red wine and pepper

SERVES 4

Preheat the oven to 180°C (350°F/Gas 4). Trim the ribs of excess fat. Heat a splash of olive oil in a large flameproof casserole dish and heat over high heat. Brown the beef in batches on all sides. Once browned, remove from the pan then you add the shallots and garlic cloves and brown those a little also. Sprinkle with the pepper, sugar and some salt and give them a stir, then add the tomatoes. Give it all a stir and bring to the boil then add the wine, bay leaves and rosemary. Return the ribs to the pan, stir it all again and bring to the boil. Put a tight-fitting lid on the casserole dish and cook in the oven until the meat is tender, about 1½–1¾ hours.

When cooked, carefully remove the ribs and shallots from the cooking liquor, strain the liquor into a clean saucepan and simmer until it has reduced to a consistency you are happy with — probably by one-half to one-third. While the sauce is reducing, trim any gristly pieces from the ribs where the bone was attached so that all you have left are lovely pieces of meat (the fat will have rendered during the cooking leaving the skin, and the bones will have fallen out during the cooking process and have been discarded when you strained the sauce). Keep the meat warm.

Divide the meat and shallots equally between the plates, stacking the pieces nicely. Spoon the sauce around and over the meat and serve with a side of green beans. You could also serve this with a mash of some kind or even some polenta, but the rib meat is juicy, rich and fine with just the beans.

2.25 kg (5 lb) beef ribs
olive oil
6 French shallots, peeled
4 garlic cloves
1 tablespoon cracked black pepper
2 teaspoons raw (demerara) sugar
400 g (14 oz) tin chopped tomatoes
750 ml (26 fl oz) bottle
    good-quality red wine
3 bay leaves
1 rosemary sprig

Emu rice-paper rolls   MAKES 24

350 g (12 oz) emu fillet, thinly sliced
  (see note)
¼ teaspoon white pepper
½ teaspoon sichuan peppercorns, dry-fried,
  then crushed using a mortar and pestle
vegetable or peanut oil, for pan-frying
24 round rice paper wrappers
1 carrot, julienned
1 Lebanese (short) cucumber,
  seeded and julienned
6 spring onions (scallions), cut into thirds,
  then thinly sliced lengthways so you
  have long matchsticks
100 g (3½ oz) enoki mushrooms, trimmed
  and pulled apart
100 g (3½ oz) bean sprouts, trimmed
100 g (3½ oz) snow pea
  (mangetout) sprouts
10 g (¼ oz/½ cup firmly packed)
  Vietnamese mint leaves

DRESSING
3 tablespoons fish sauce
3 tablespoons lime juice
1 red bird's eye chilli, chopped
1 tablespoon grated palm sugar (jaggery)

DIPPING SAUCE
1 tablespoon sesame oil
3 tablespoons hoisin sauce

For the dressing: Mix all the ingredients together in a small bowl.

For the dipping sauce: Mix the ingredients together in a small bowl.

Season the sliced emu with the white pepper, sichuan pepper and some salt. Add a splash of oil to a frying pan or wok and heat over high heat. Add the slices of meat and cook briefly to sear — (it will continue to cook after you remove it from the heat), set aside.

Soak the rice paper wrappers a few at a time in water until soft. Take them out of the water and stick the top edge to the edge of a bench and let them hang there for a couple of minutes — this will make them more elastic.

Mix all the other ingredients together in a large bowl and then very lightly cover with the dressing.

Place a rice paper wrapper on the bench and lay a slice or two of the emu in the middle of the roll, then layer a small amount of the dressed vegetables on top of the emu — do not overfill. Fold the left edge over the emu and vegetables and then fold the top down and the bottom up so that they stick to the left folded edge. Now roll to the right trying to keep the roll firm so that the filling is tightly tucked inside. If you have done it right you should have a tightly rolled mini spring roll type shape. Serve with the dipping sauce.

If you can't get emu then try making these with kangaroo fillet, or some good old regular steak.

You can either buy squid-ink pasta or you can make your own. There are many different pasta recipes out there to try so have a look around in books to find one that works for you. Following is the pasta recipe I used in the show which was given to me by Shaun Morris, the then head chef of Berardos Restaurant at Noosa.

Spanner crab with squid-ink angel hair pasta

SERVES 4

Cook the crab claws in boiling salted water for 4 minutes then remove and plunge into iced water. Crack the claws and remove the meat. Set the claw meat aside until the pasta and sauce are ready to serve.

Gently fry the garlic and chilli in the olive oil for a few minutes, then add the crabmeat and cook for a few minutes, being careful not to overcook. Add the white wine and half the parsley and cook for a few minutes more until the flavours are combined, then season with salt and freshly ground black pepper.

Cook the pasta in boiling salted water, stirring occasionally so it doesn't stick, until al dente. Drain well and add the pasta to the frying pan with the crab. Mix it through thoroughly with tongs to coat the pasta with the sauce.

To serve, divide the pasta, crabmeat and sauce equally between four plates and sprinkle with the remaining parsley. Top with the meat from the crab claw, then garnish with the salmon roe.

4 raw spanner crab claws
1 garlic clove, finely chopped
1 red chilli, finely chopped
2 tablespoons olive oil
300 g (10½ oz) raw spanner crabmeat
125 ml (4 fl oz/½ cup) dry white wine
2 tablespoons finely chopped flat-leaf (Italian) parsley
400 g (14 oz) squid-ink angel hair pasta
2 teaspoons salmon roe

This pasta works equally well with prawns (shrimp) or squid or beautiful, fresh plump scallops. In fact, why don't you treat yourself and use all of the above for a wonderful seafood medley.

Veal roulades with beetroot and radish salad

SERVES 4

Preheat the oven to 220°C (425°F/Gas 7). Lay the potato, flat side down, with its long edge towards you. Starting on the right side, make a slice across the short side of the potato, without slicing all the way to the bottom. Continue making slices at 2 mm (1/16 inch) intervals all the way to the left side of the potato. Repeat with the other potato pieces. Season with some olive oil, salt and paprika and roast for 20–30 minutes, or until crisp and golden. Remove from the oven and keep warm. Reduce the oven temperature to 180°C (350°F/Gas 4).

While the potato is cooking, lay the pieces of veal on a bench and, if necessary, flatten them out so they are of uniform thickness and size. Put them between two sheets of plastic wrap and gently hammer with a mallet or rolling pin. They should be about the size and thickness of a CD case.

Place a layer of spinach over the veal, followed by 2–3 slices of cheese, then place 2–3 pieces of semi-dried tomato in the middle of the veal. Place 2–3 sage leaves on the tomato and then lay two spears of asparagus over the top.

Carefully roll the veal tightly so that one side just overlaps the other, then use cocktail sticks to secure. Lay a piece of prosciutto on the bench on the diagonal then place the veal roll on top and roll — because the prosciutto is on the angle it will wrap around and along the veal roulade. Brown the roulades in an ovenproof frying pan with a touch of olive oil turning so as not to overcook then put the pan in the oven for 7–8 minutes. Remove from the pan and keep warm while you make the sauce.

Add the Madeira and the butter to the juices in the pan. Mix and season with salt and pepper to taste then reduce over medium heat to your desired consistency.

To make the salad: grate the beetroot and radishes into a bowl — you need about a cup of each for four people. Splash with the olive oil and vinegar, season with salt and pepper and mix well.

Serve the roulade with some salad and potato and drizzle the veal with the sauce.

2 potatoes, peeled and halved lengthways
olive oil
½ teaspoon paprika
4 pieces veal schnitzel
2 large handfuls baby English spinach
8–12 very thin slices gruyère cheese
8–12 semi-dried (sun-blushed) tomatoes
8–12 sage leaves
8 asparagus spears
4 prosciutto slices
3 tablespoons Madeira
30 g (1 oz) butter

BEETROOT AND RADISH SALAD
1 large beetroot (beet), peeled
8 radishes, peeled
2 tablespoons olive oil
1 tablespoon sherry vinegar

It might seem like a little bit of trouble but believe me, it isn't. If I cook this for friends I usually ask my mate to get up and help me layer and roll — that way the girls can either look on and laugh or be impressed!

There are many recipes for damper and it's actually very easy to make. However, since I was cooking in the traditional home of damper — the outback — I wanted to make something a little different to the norm and used native bush spices. I bought my spices from Herbie's Spices in Sydney, www.herbies.com.au, and, as they deliver anywhere in the world, you can get them too! All the spices Herbie's sell are of great quality and are the real deal whether they come from country Australia or the middle of Africa.

I used Coopers Stout as it is one of my favourite beers to cook with and in this case, it suits the damper perfectly. The roasted character of the beer goes with the toasted wattle seeds. The malt works with the sweetness of the bush tomato and the bitterness in the beer complements the spiciness of the pepperleaf.

Aussie beer bush damper

SERVES 6 AS A SIDE

375 g (13 oz/2½ cups) self-raising flour
1 teaspoon salt
3 teaspoons ground akudjura
(see note)
2 teaspoons ground mountain pepperleaf
(see note, page 15)
½ teaspoon toasted ground wattle seeds
about 185 ml (6 fl oz/¾ cup) Coopers Best
Extra Stout or other stout

Preheat the oven to 200°C (400°F/Gas 6). Mix all of the dry ingredients together in a bowl and then gradually pour in the beer — you may need to use another 50 ml (1½ fl oz) if the mixture is too dry. Mix with a wooden spoon until the dough comes together. Turn out of the bowl and knead for several minutes until it is smooth. Form the dough into a round loaf shape about 15 cm (6 inches) in diameter. Put the loaf on a sheet of baking paper on a baking tray or wire rack, and score the top of the loaf into six wedges. Spray with water and cook for 30–40 minutes. The damper is ready when it is crispy on the outside and sounds hollow when tapped. Turn out onto a wire rack and allow to cool or rip it apart straight away, slather it in butter and eat with a cup of tea!

Akudjura is a native Australian bush tomato with a caramel-like taste that complements both sweet and savoury foods.

Crocodile and mango curry

SERVES 4

Preheat the oven to 180°C (350°F/Gas 4). In a flameproof casserole dish, sweat the onion and capsicum in a splash of vegetable or peanut oil until almost starting to go golden, then add the curry paste and cook for a minute or two. Add the crocodile and mix well to coat the meat, then add the tamarind paste. Cook over high heat for a couple of minutes, stirring constantly. Mix in the mango pulp, then add the coconut milk, lime leaves and lemongrass stem.

Transfer to the oven and cook for about 35 minutes, adding the vegetables after about 20 minutes.

Stir through some coriander and then serve in a big bowl on some basmati rice. Garnish with the remaining coriander.

1 red onion, sliced

½ red capsicum (pepper), cut into thin strips

vegetable or peanut oil

1 tablespoon ready-made red curry paste

500 g (1 lb 2 oz) crocodile meat, diced
(available from gourmet butchers)

1 tablespoon tamarind paste

375 g (13 oz/2½ cups) fresh mango pulp
(see note)

400 g (14 oz) tin coconut milk

4 makrut (kaffir lime) leaves

1 lemongrass stem, bruised

16 snow peas (mangetout), trimmed

16 green beans, trimmed

2 baby eggplants (aubergines), cut into
1 cm (½ inch) thick rounds

1 handful of chopped coriander
(cilantro) leaves

If you can't buy fresh mangoes then buy some frozen cheeks from a greengrocer and thaw them out — when thawed, put them in the blender and blitz them to a pulp.

Gado gado

SERVES 2

2 potatoes, quartered

300 g (10½ oz) pumpkin (winter squash), cut into pieces the same size as the potato quarters

300 g (10½ oz) orange sweet potato, cut into pieces the same size as the potato quarters

16 green beans, trimmed

60 g (2¼ oz/1 cup) broccoli florets

250 g (9 oz) firm tofu, sliced into 2.5 cm (1 inch) squares

rice flour, for dusting

vegetable or peanut oil, for frying

5 spring onions (scallions), thinly sliced

150 g (5½ oz/2 cups) very thinly sliced cabbage

135 g (4¾ oz/1 cup) peeled and julienned zucchini (courgette)

125 g (4½ oz/1 cup) cauliflower florets

3 boiled eggs, quartered

PEANUT SAUCE

2½ tablespoons crunchy peanut butter

100 ml (3½ fl oz) banana liqueur (optional)

3 tablespoons water

2 tablespoons kecap manis

2 teaspoons sambal oelek

¼ teaspoon chipotle flakes or smoked paprika

juice of 1 lime

For the sauce: Put the peanut butter into a small saucepan over gentle heat, add the liqueur and water and then mix through until all the peanut butter is mixed and broken down into a paste — add more liqueur if needed. Add the kecap manis, sambal oelek and chipotle flakes and mix through, then add the lime juice. Taste and adjust for flavour as per your own taste buds.

Put the potato, pumpkin and sweet potato into a saucepan full of salted boiling water and cook until tender — be careful not to overcook as you want them to keep their integrity in the salad. Blanch the beans and broccoli in boiling water until slightly softened but still firm to the bite. (I put them in a sieve and drop that into the same pan as the potatoes, pumpkin and sweet potatoes.) Drain.

Meanwhile, lightly dust the tofu in rice flour. Add a splash of oil to a frying pan and fry the tofu over medium–high heat for 5 minutes turning occasionally or until golden. Drain on paper towel. Add a little more oil to the pan and cook the spring onions until crispy. Drain on paper towel.

Put the raw cabbage, zucchini and cauliflower into a large bowl and give them a good mix to combine them all. Add the still-warm beans, broccoli, potato, pumpkin and sweet potato and give it all another mix. Pour three-quarters of the peanut sauce into the bowl and mix well, making sure all the vegetables are evenly coated.

Divide the vegetables equally between two plates, arrange the tofu around the bottom of the salad and the egg quarters on top. Garnish with a good pinch of the crispy shallots and drizzle the remaining sauce over the salad and around the plate.

This dish originated in Positano and was created to celebrate summer, with its rich colours representing freshness and vitality. If you can't find squid-ink pasta, you can use fresh squid ink — add a little to the dish during cooking. If you want to add some chillies do so moderately so you don't overpower the sweetness of the recipe. Use a nice bottle of pinot grigio, preferably Italian — what isn't used in the recipe can be served alongside the pasta.

Linguette ai fiori

RECIPE BY TONY PERCUOCO FROM RISTORANTE FELLINI, GOLD COAST

SERVES 4

400 g (14 oz) squid-ink dried linguette
    or fettuccine

olive oil

150 g (5½ oz) raw prawns (shrimp),
    peeled and deveined

150 g (5½ oz) squid tubes, cleaned
    and sliced

3 garlic cloves, sliced

100 g (3½ oz) zucchini
    (courgette), sliced

3 roma (plum) tomatoes, seeded and
    chopped (I love san marzano tomatoes)

1 red chilli, sliced (optional)

90 ml (3 fl oz) dry white wine

1 small handful flat-leaf (Italian)
    parsley, chopped

12 zucchini (courgette) flowers,
    roughly torn

4 tablespoons extra virgin olive oil

Fill a large saucepan with plenty of water and add a very generous pinch of salt. Bring the water to the boil and add the pasta giving it a stir so that it separates and doesn't stick together. Stir every 5 minutes and check for readiness by tasting the pasta. You want it to be al dente, literally 'to the tooth', which means that when you bite the pasta there is a tiny bit of resistance in the centre of the pasta. Tip the water and pasta into a colander and drain. Do not rinse the pasta as you will wash away starch and flavour. Pour a splash of oil into a large heavy-based frying pan and heat over high heat. When the oil is hot, add the prawns, squid and some salt and cook for a few minutes. Add the garlic, zucchini, tomato and a little more salt and cook for a further 2 minutes. You can add chilli if you prefer a slightly hotter dish.

Deglaze the pan with the wine and cook for a further 3 minutes or until the liquid is hot. Add the drained pasta to the pan, stirring frequently. Sprinkle with the chopped parsley, add the zucchini flowers last (otherwise they will turn bitter) and half the amount of extra virgin olive oil and mix together well.

Serve on individual large flat plates or a platter, drizzle the remaining oil around the plate and serve. And please under no circumstances is this dish to have parmesan cheese. Buon appetito.

Barramundi on a bed of lentils

SERVES 2

Heat a splash of olive oil in a large saucepan and cook the onion over medium heat for a few minutes until sweated down a little then add the carrot, celery and garlic and fry until softened. Add the diced pancetta and cook until browned, then add the lentils, rosemary and enough chicken stock to cover. Simmer for 30–45 minutes, stirring occasionally and adding more stock as needed until the lentils are cooked. Just when you think the lentils are cooked, add the tomato and cook for a few minutes more. Taste and season with salt and pepper.

Season the barramundi with salt and black pepper and then fry in a mix of some olive oil and the butter to add a slightly richer quality to the cooked fish. Fry flesh side down first to get good colour on the fillet, then turn and fry the skin side.

Serve the lentils on a warmed plate and top with two fillets of barramundi. Drizzle a little extra virgin olive oil over to finish.

olive oil
1 onion, finely diced
1 carrot, chopped
2 celery stalks, chopped
2 garlic cloves, finely chopped
100 g (3½ oz) pancetta, diced
185 g (6½ oz/1 cup) brown or
    green lentils
2 rosemary sprigs
1.5 litres (52 fl oz/6 cups) chicken stock
4 small tomatoes, halved and then cut
    in thirds
4 barramundi fillets, about 120 g
    (4¼ oz) each
20 g (¾ oz) butter
extra virgin olive oil, for drizzling

I first cooked this dish at a restaurant in Townsville called The Watermark. They liked it so much they put it on their menu!

Coconut-braised beef in jungle curry

RECIPE BY ANNETTE FEAR OF THE SPIRIT HOUSE, YANDINA

SERVES 6

BRAISED BEEF
½ teaspoon white peppercorns
3 coriander (cilantro) roots
3 garlic cloves
500 ml (17 fl oz/2 cups) coconut cream
2 tablespoons fish sauce
2 tablespoons grated palm
    sugar (jaggery)
500 g (1 lb 2 oz) boneless beef shin

JUNGLE CURRY PASTE
8 green bird's eye chillies, chopped
2 large green chillies, seeded
    and chopped
5 cm (2 inch) piece of galangal,
    peeled and chopped
2 lemongrass stems, thinly sliced
1 tablespoon krachai (wild
    ginger), chopped

4 French shallots, peeled and chopped
9 garlic cloves, peeled
½ teaspoon makrut (kaffir lime) zest
2 cm (¾ inch) piece fresh turmeric,
    peeled and chopped
1 teaspoon salt

CURRY
2 tablespoons vegetable oil
2–3 tablespoons jungle curry paste
250 ml (9 fl oz/1 cup) chicken stock
    or water
2 tablespoons krachai (wild ginger)
110 g (3¾ oz) baby corn,
    sliced lengthways
125 g (4½ oz/1 cup) sliced snake
    (yard-long) beans
2 tablespoons fish sauce
1 tablespoon grated palm sugar (jaggery)
4 double makrut (kaffir lime) leaves
15 g (½ oz/½ cup) Thai basil

GARNISH
2 tablespoons coconut cream
2 tablespoons ready-made
    crisp-fried shallots
1 long red chilli, seeded and cut into strips
coriander (cilantro) sprigs

For the braised beef: Grind the white peppercorns using a mortar and pestle, add the coriander and garlic and pound to a paste. Place in a heavy-based saucepan over medium heat with the coconut cream, fish sauce and palm sugar, stir to combine and bring to the boil. Add the beef shin and simmer for 2 hours, or until the meat is tender. Allow the meat to cool in the coconut cream. Remove and slice the meat into 2.5 cm (1 inch) medallions.

For the jungle curry paste: Combine all the ingredients using a mortar and pestle and pound to a paste.

For the curry: Heat the oil in a wok over high heat and cook the curry paste until fragrant. Add the stock, sliced beef, krachai, baby corn and snake beans and stir-fry for 1 minute. Stir in the fish sauce, palm sugar, Thai basil and makrut leaves. Simmer until the meat has warmed through.

Transfer to a serving bowl, spoon over the coconut cream and garnish with shallots, chilli strips and coriander sprigs.

Prawn, avocado and bocconcini pizza

SERVES 2

PIZZA SAUCE
olive oil
1 onion, finely chopped
2 garlic cloves, finely chopped
2–3 tablespoons tomato paste
   (concentrated purée)
2 x 400 g (14 oz) tins chopped tomatoes
125 ml (4 fl oz/½ cup) water
pinch of oregano

PIZZA DOUGH (FOR 4 PIZZAS)
pinch of sugar
2½ teaspoons olive oil
230 ml (7¾ fl oz) warm water
2 teaspoons dried yeast
400 g (14 oz/2⅔) '00' flour
   (see note, page 29)
½ teaspoon salt

TOPPING (FOR 1 PIZZA)
2 garlic cloves, crushed and soaked in
   3 tablespoons olive oil
about 4 tablespoons pizza sauce
1 handful of basil leaves
6 bocconcini (fresh baby mozzarella
   cheese) balls, sliced
12 raw prawns (shrimp), peeled,
   deveined, and tails removed
1 avocado, sliced
pinch of chilli powder or dried chilli flakes
grated parmesan cheese

For the pizza sauce: Heat a splash of olive oil in a saucepan over medium heat. Fry the onion and garlic until translucent, then add the tomato paste and fry for a couple of minutes. Add the tomato, water and oregano and bring to the boil, season with salt and pepper. Simmer for 30 minutes. This makes enough for six pizzas — store the leftover in the fridge for up to 1 week or freeze it.

For the pizza dough: Put the sugar and a splash of olive oil into the warm water and then add the yeast. Give it a stir and let it sit for 10 minutes while the yeast gets itself going. Put the flour in a large bowl and mix in the salt. Slowly add the yeasty water to the flour and mix until you get a ball of dough — you may or may not use all the water; if you do use it all and not all the flour is combined then just add some more water to the dough. Turn the dough out on to a floured kitchen bench and give it a good kneading for 10 minutes until you feel the texture change to a smooth consistency.

Get another bowl large enough to fit the dough, spray with olive oil and sprinkle flour. Put the dough in the bowl — and cover the top with plastic wrap that you have sprayed and floured. Put the bowl in a warm place and let the dough rise for as long as it takes, 1–1½ hours.

When the dough has risen take it out of the bowl, roll it into a log and cut into six equal portions. Roll each portion into a ball, dust with flour and cover with a tea towel (dish cloth) until ready to roll out into a pizza base.

Preheat your oven to its highest setting. Brush a 30 cm (12 inch) pizza pan with the crushed garlic olive oil. Roll out one portion of your dough and place on the pizza pan. Brush the outside of the dough (which becomes the crust) with the same olive oil. Prebake the pizza base until it starts to colour and become slightly crisp, remove it from the oven. Lightly cover the pizza base with the sauce. Lay the basil leaves around the base. Top with the bocconcini, raw prawns followed by slices of avocado in between the prawns. Sprinkle with the chilli powder and then lightly sprinkle freshly grated parmesan cheese over the top. Finally, using a pastry brush or a spoon flick or dot the garlic and oil mixture around the pizza to add that last bit of flavour.

Return the pizza to the oven and cook for 8–10 minutes, or until the prawns are cooked to your liking. Remove from the oven and eat!

Spiced barramundi with a Moroccan carrot dressing, red claw, avocado and smoked salmon stack

RECIPE BY MATT MERRIN FROM THE WATERMARK, TOWNSVILLE

SERVES 4

For the spicy marinade: Roughly chop the coriander. Roast the spices lightly for 2 minutes in the oven at 160°C (315°F/Gas 2–3). Combine all the ingredients. Marinate the barramundi in the mixture for a couple of hours.

For the dressing: Pour the orange juice into a small saucepan over medium heat and reduce to 50 ml (1½ fl oz). Add the diced carrot, orange blossom water and baharat and boil over medium heat until the carrot is very soft. Blitz with a stick blender. The sauce consistency should coat the back of a spoon.

Heat a large frying pan with a splash of oil, and place the fillets in the pan. Cook until golden brown and turn over. This will only take a few minutes on each side.

While the barramundi is cooking, mould the avocado into a 7.5 cm (3 inch) round cutter on the side of four serving plates, pushing down the avocado gently to hold its shape. Place a piece of smoked salmon on top of each avocado stack. Cut the red claw in half and place two halves on top of each stack.

Drizzle a little carrot dressing in the centre of each plate and place the barramundi over it. Garnish with lemon, and a small piece of chervil, then season the fish with sea salt.

olive oil
8 x 100 g (3½ oz) barramundi fillets
2 avocados, diced
150 g (5½ oz) smoked salmon
4 x 50 g (1¾ oz) cooked red claw or large prawns (shrimp)
100 ml (3½ fl oz) Moroccan carrot dressing (see below)
lemon wedges, to garnish
chervil, to garnish

SPICY MARINADE
½ bunch coriander (cilantro)
½ teaspoon paprika
½ teaspoon ground cinnamon
½ teaspoon cayenne pepper
½ teaspoon ground cumin
½ teaspoon cracked black pepper
½ teaspoon allspice
1 garlic clove, finely chopped
zest and juice of 1 lemon
50 ml (1½ fl oz) olive oil

MOROCCAN CARROT DRESSING
100 ml (3½ fl oz) orange juice
¼ large carrot, finely diced
¼ teaspoon orange blossom water
pinch of baharat (Middle Eastern spice mix)

I reckon this is a great share plate for two; however, you could serve it up on two plates and add more pineapple and banana as you see fit, not forgetting to add a good scoop of ice cream. Now, if you want to make this for four, then just cook this recipe twice, remembering to include one pineapple ring per person.

Flamed banana and pineapple with passionfruit ice cream

SERVES 2

30 g (1 oz) unsalted butter

1 large firm banana, halved crossways, then halved lengthways

1 ring of pineapple, about 8 mm (⅜ inch) thick, core removed

1 tablespoon roughly chopped mint, plus extra, to garnish

1 cinnamon stick

1 splash of Malibu

ICE CREAM

125 ml (4 fl oz/½ cup) milk

1 egg

165 g (5¾ oz) caster (superfine) sugar

500 ml (17 fl oz/2 cups) cream

250 g (9 oz/1 cup) passionfruit pulp

Flaming the fruit adds an extra bit of flavour and raises this dish from a kid's treat to an outstanding adult dessert.

For the ice cream: Mix all the ingredients together making sure the sugar is dissolved, then put into an ice-cream maker and churn until it reaches the desired consistency. Freeze until solid.

For the fruit: Heat the butter in a frying pan or wok over medium heat and, once it starts to foam, add the banana, pineapple ring, mint and cinnamon stick. Cook until brown and caramelised on both sides of the fruit. Then take a ladle, pour some Malibu into it and hold over a flame, gently heating the liquor. It will eventually catch alight and begin to burn; when this happens pour the liquor over the fruit and watch as it 'flames'.

Place the pineapple ring on a plate and then stack the banana quarters on top two first and then the other two on top and crossing like building a stack of wood. Carefully place a scoop of the passionfruit ice cream on top of this stack and garnish with a little more mint.

NORTHERN TERRITORY & WESTERN AUSTRALIA

I am wondering how in a paragraph or two I can do justice to these regions. I can't. You just have to go there and I guarantee you will be blown away and satisfied beyond belief. I might even bump into you.

I grew up in Fremantle, Western Australia and loved it. Fremantle is a port city and back in the early days it was a pretty rough old place, but thanks to the America's Cup coming to town in the 1980s, 'Freo', as we like to call it, was transformed into a historic port town with markets, pubs, cafés and great alfresco restaurants. My mum still lives there so I visit a fair bit and always do the same things. First, I go to town for a really good coffee at one of the many great Italian coffee shops — some of them have been there since I was a kid. Then Mum and I stroll around the Freo markets and buy some fresh salad and vegetables and check out what the local artists are doing. Then we walk over to Fishing Boat Harbour and pop into Little Creatures Brewing company for a pint of ale and tapas for lunch. After that, we wander over to Sealanes fish market and pick out some local fish like Nannygai and maybe some local prawns and then go to my brother's house and cook up a feast. See why I like going home to Freo?

Occasionally I get down to Margaret River which offers an absolute smorgasbord of fantastic foodstuffs, some of the best wineries in the world, a plethora of micro-breweries, amazing produce shops and equally impressive restaurants and chefs.

As for the Northern Territory — I was a little frantic, I was a little lost, the directions were wrong and the doors were locked. I banged on them and pressed my nose to the glass hoping to spy someone and get them to unlock the doors. I finally made my way around to the back of the cooking school, found a door ajar and let myself in. I could hear a voice down the corridor, which I followed and finally found a big bloke sitting behind a desk talking on the phone. He looked me up and down and I could tell he wasn't impressed with what he was looking at. He hung up the phone and said in his booming voice, 'You're late; if you worked for me you would be out on your arse,' and that was my first meeting with the Walkabout Chef, Steve Sunk. We had a great time cooking together. He made smoked kangaroo and crocodile; I made him fruit soup with feta cheese. He wasn't impressed and told me so — I reckon we'll be friends for life!

It's the people you meet that so often cement a great meal or food experience in your memory. I have been very lucky to meet some truly inspirational people — Steve is one of them and he is just like the food and produce of the Northern Territory — big, bold and brash.

I love barramundi but I have always bought it wild as often the farmed variety can taste a bit muddy. But since tasting Humpty Doo barramundi, I have changed my mind. So much so, that I am asking my fishmonger to order it in for me. After Jimmy Shu (the chef I cooked with in this episode) tasted my dish he declared the same and said he was going to talk to Humpty Doo about getting it for his restaurants.

Chinese-style steamed barramundi

SERVES 2

Choose a heatproof plate large enough to fit the fish and line it with the Chinese cabbage leaves. Sprinkle half of the sliced spring onions, bamboo shoots and thinly sliced ginger over the cabbage leaves.

Cut three diagonal slits into the flesh of the fish down to the bone and then cut three more in the opposite direction to form a diamond pattern on the side. Do the same to the other side of the fish. Sprinkle a little salt and the sugar over both sides of the fish and then lay the fish on top of the plate lined with Chinese cabbage. Put the julienned ginger inside the cavity of the fish.

Combine the sesame oil and soy sauce then pour the mixture over the fish. Place the plate in a large steamer basket and steam for about 15 minutes. To test if the fish is done, take a knife and place the tip between the flesh and the bone and gently lift upward — if the flesh comes away easily the fish is cooked.

Remove the fish from the steamer, place on a heatproof serving plate and garnish with the remaining spring onions, bamboo shoots and thinly sliced ginger, and also the thinly sliced red chilli. Heat the peanut oil in a small saucepan until smoking hot, then carefully pour the oil over the top of the fish. Garnish with the red and yellow capsicum, the chopped coriander, the lime juice and a drizzle of soy sauce.

4 Chinese cabbage (wong bok) leaves
8 spring onions (scallions), thinly sliced
220 g (7¾ oz) tin bamboo shoots, drained and thinly sliced
7 cm (2¾ inch) piece fresh ginger, thinly sliced
1 whole barramundi or any firm white-fleshed fish, about 800 g (1 lb 12 oz), scaled, gutted and cleaned
½ teaspoon caster (superfine) sugar
2 tablespoons soy sauce
5 cm (2 inch) piece of fresh ginger, julienned
3 teaspoons sesame oil
2 long red chillies, thinly sliced
4 tablespoons peanut oil
¼ red capsicum (pepper), very finely julienned
¼ yellow capsicum (pepper), very finely julienned
1 handful of coriander (cilantro) leaves, chopped
juice of ½ bush lime or regular lime

Buffalo sausage

MAKES 2 CUMBERLAND SAUSAGES SERVES 8

2 red onions, chopped

olive oil

5 garlic cloves

500 g (1 lb 2 oz) minced (ground) pork fat

250 g (9 oz) minced (ground) pork

110 g (3¾ oz/¾ cup) pistachio nuts, finely chopped in a food processor

1.5 kg (3 lb 5 oz) coarsely minced (ground) buffalo

2 tablespoons finely chopped rosemary

1 tablespoon finely chopped thyme

225 g (8 oz/1½ cups) sun-dried tomatoes, finely chopped

1½ tablespoons salt

2 teaspoons white pepper

125 ml (4 fl oz/½ cup) James Squire Porter

5 metres sausage casings, 43 mm (1¾ inch) bungs (ask your butcher)

juice of ½ lemon

olive oil

> James Squire beers are readily available around Australia — Porter is a style that many micro breweries are now making — but if you can't find one, then you can substitute with any variety of stout.

Preheat the oven to 160°C (315°F/Gas 2–3). Place the onions in a roasting tin and drizzle with olive oil. Peel the garlic and wrap in foil with a splash of olive oil. Put in the tin with the onions and roast for 15 minutes or until cooked. Process the garlic and onion in a food processor to a rough paste.

It is important to have your meat very cold as during the mixing process it will warm up and could be susceptible to bacteria. Mix the pork fat and pork meat thoroughly through the buffalo meat using your hands to really work it all together. Add the onion and garlic purée, pistachio nuts, rosemary, thyme, tomato, salt and pepper and thoroughly mix all of the ingredients. Add the beer and again give the mixture a good mix. The sausage casings normally come dried and packed in salt so you need to remove some of them from the packet and soak in cold water. Drain and refill with fresh water and soak again, three or four times. Then take an end of the casing, stretch it over your tap and run cold water through the entire length to clean the inside of the casing. Lastly let the skin soak in clean cold water with the lemon juice. You will probably have to cut lengths of the casing as they often get into knots so for each round of sausage you will want about a 1–1.5 metre (3–5 foot) length of casing.

Using a sausage stuffing machine thread your casing onto the filling nozzle, tying a knot in the end of the skin. Stuff the skin with half the sausage mix; when you get to the end of the casing or feel that the sausage is long enough (remember that we are making a Cumberland-style which is one long coil of sausage), tie a knot in the tail end. Tightly coil the sausage and using a wooden skewer pierce through the tail end of the sausage right through the centre and out the other side and then repeat with another skewer a quarter of the way around the sausage so that the skewers form a cross and the sausage is held together. Repeat with another sausage casing and the rest of the filling. Keep in the fridge for a day or two to firm the sausages.

Fry the sausage 'coil' in hot oil in a frying pan large enough to hold the whole sausage or fry on the hotplate of your barbecue. Prick the sausage with a skewer to release some of the fat and to try and avoid it splitting.

Capsicum and porter relish

MAKES ABOUT 250 ML (9 FL OZ/1 CUP)

To prepare the capsicum, slice the sides from the core so you have four flat sides from each capsicum and place them, skin side up, under a hot grill (broiler). Let them blister and burn until blackened and then place them in a plastic bag to sweat for 5 minutes. Peel the skins off and roughly chop the flesh.

Heat a frying pan over medium–high heat then add some olive oil. When the oil is hot add the onion, chilli and garlic to the pan and fry for 5–8 minutes, stirring often so the mixture doesn't burn. Add the tomato and cook for several minutes, then season with the salt and the pepper. Toss in the capsicum and give it all a good mix through and cook for a further 2–3 minutes. Pour in the beer and the Worcestershire and cook the liquid down for another 5 minutes. The more you cook out the liquid from the beer and Worcestershire the firmer the relish will be. Taste for seasoning then pour the mixture into a blender and pulse. You can either leave it chunky or blend it to a smooth paste.

2 red capsicums (peppers)
olive oil
1 red onion, roughly chopped
2 long red chillies, roughly chopped
5 garlic cloves, roughly chopped
2 tomatoes, roughly chopped
½ x 330 ml (11¼ fl oz) bottle James Squire Porter (see note page 80)
2–3 tablespoons Worcestershire sauce

This relish is good with everything — sausages, steak, burgers, polenta and chips or even spread on sourdough with chicken for a tasty sandwich. I probably wouldn't put it on my ice cream …

Venison pie   SERVES 8-10

olive oil

½ red onion, diced

2 garlic cloves, finely chopped

40 g (1½ oz) smoked bacon, cut
    into lardons

2 teaspoons each of finely chopped
    rosemary, sage, thyme and marjoram

1 kg (2 lb 4 oz) venison chuck steak, cut
    into 3 cm cubes

60 g (2¼ oz/½ cup) plain
    (all-purpose) flour

½ teaspoon paprika

175 ml (5½ fl oz) Bootleg Brewery Toms
    Amber Ale or other amber ale

125 ml (4 fl oz/½ cup) veal stock

3 roma (plum) tomatoes, quartered and
    then halved

60 g (2¼ oz/½ cup) sultanas (golden raisins)

½ eggplant (aubergine), cubed

1 sheet of ready-made puff pastry

beetroot chutney, to serve

SOUR CREAM PASTRY

300 g (10½ oz/2 cups) plain
    (all-purpose) flour

175 g (6 oz) unsalted butter, chopped

175 g (6 oz) sour cream

EGG WASH

1 egg

2 tablespoons milk

Preheat the oven to 180°C (350°F/Gas 4). Heat a large flameproof casserole dish over medium heat. Cook the onion in a splash of oil until translucent, add the garlic and bacon and cook for 5 minutes, add the herbs and remove from the pan.

Meanwhile, put the flour into a resealable plastic bag and season with salt, pepper and the paprika. Put the venison in the bag and shake to coat.

Add more oil to the casserole dish and brown the venison in batches, shaking off any excess flour before adding to the pan and adding more olive oil for each batch.

Return all the meat to the pan along with the onion mixture. Pour in the beer and bring to the boil, then add the veal stock and bring back to the boil. Season with salt and pepper. Cover with a lid and put into the oven for 50 minutes.

Meanwhile, for the sour cream pastry, in an electric mixer, mix the flour, butter and a pinch of salt until it resembles breadcrumbs, add the sour cream and mix until it forms a dough. Remove from the mixer (do not knead), wrap in plastic wrap and rest in the fridge for 30 minutes.

Check the meat and add the tomato, sultanas and eggplant and cook for a further 40 minutes or until the meat is tender and pulls apart easily. If you still have a lot of liquid in the pan, remove all the solids and reduce the sauce on the stove until it is thick. Remove from the heat, return the meat to the sauce and allow to cool.

Meanwhile, lightly grease a 22 cm (8½ inch) spring-form cake tin. On a lightly floured surface, roll out the dough to 5 mm (¼ inch) thick. Line the tin with the sour cream pastry, gently pressing into the base and sides of the tin, leaving the excess pastry hanging over the edges. Place a piece of baking paper over the pastry and fill it with uncooked beans or rice. Bake for 20 minutes then remove the paper and beans and bake for a further 15–25 minutes, or until the pastry is golden. Remove from the oven and cool slightly. Trim the excess pastry from the edges and fill with the pie mixture.

For the egg wash, whisk together the egg and the milk. Cut a circle from the puff pastry to fit over the edges of the pie. Brush sides of sour cream pastry with egg wash so that the pastry lid will seal onto it. Press edges to seal and trim any excess pastry. Brush the lid with egg wash and cut a cross into the centre for the steam to escape. Cook for about 30 minutes or until golden brown. Serve with some beetroot chutney.

Smoked kangaroo pastrami

RECIPES BY STEVEN SUNK, THE WALKABOUT CHEF

SERVES 6 AS A STARTER

1 kg (1 lb 2 oz) kangaroo rump, cut into
    4 equal size pieces
3 cups of Hickory smoking chips

TANAMI BUSH CHUTNEY
½ cup each of dried pear, dried apricots,
    dates, dried apples and sultanas
    (golden raisins)
300 g (10½ oz/2 cups) bush limes or
    regular limes, chopped
60 g (2¼ oz/½ cup) akudjura (see page 62)
1 red onion, roughly chopped
375 g (13 oz/2 cups) soft brown sugar
500 ml (17 fl oz/2 cups) red wine vinegar
    or cider vinegar
½ teaspoon freshly grated nutmeg
½ teaspoon ground ginger

CURING SOLUTION
3 litres (105 fl oz) water
200 g (7 oz) salt
75 g (2½ oz) soft brown sugar
2 teaspoons peppercorns
2 bay leaves

For the chutney: Dice all the dried fruits except the sultanas and put them all in a large bowl. Add the limes and akudjura. Fill the bowl with enough water to just cover, then soak overnight.

Do not drain the fruits. Add the remainder of the ingredients and transfer to a large saucepan. Bring to the boil then lower the heat and simmer for 1 hour or until it thickens. Taste for sugar as bush limes are strong in flavour. Process the chutney with a stick blender or you can leave it chunky if you prefer. Pour the chutney into sterilised jars.

While still hot, seal with sterilised lids and leave to mature in a cool, dry place for about 6–8 weeks before use.

For the curing solution: Place the water in a non reactive container. Stir in the salt and sugar and mix until they dissolve. Add the peppercorns and bay leaves. Add the kangaroo pieces to the solution and cover with baking paper. Place in the refrigerator for 5–6 days — this should be enough time to cure the meat. Remove the kangaroo from the solution and wash in fresh water then dry with paper towel.

To smoke the meat, preheat your barbecue grill to high. Place the smoking chips in the smoking box and put a rack on top. Then put the kangaroo on the rack, cover with the lid and put on the barbecue. Keep the heat high enough to smoke the meat for 15–25 minutes or until the meat is coloured.

Keep an eye on the smoking process, you don't want the smoking mix to burn — just smoke.

Remove and set aside to cool. Cut into thin slices and serve with the tanami bush chutney.

Smoking boxes and smoking chips are available from barbecue, hardware and camping stores.

I like to cook prawns this way as the caramelisation works beautifully with the salt and smokiness from the barbecue. This amount of prawns could serve just one person if you love prawns cooked like this as much as I do but I would suggest sharing this with at least a friend or three.

Barbecued prawns

SERVES 1-4 AS A STARTER

Peel the garlic and then crush into the olive oil and let sit for an hour or two. Peel and devein the prawns, leaving their tails intact. Add the salt and chilli powder (if you want a little background heat) to the oil and give it a stir and then pour over the prawns and give them a really good mix.

Cook over high heat on the grill of your barbecue or in a chargrill pan for a few minutes each side until cooked.

Put the prawns in a bowl and serve with wedges of lemon and some napkins and, of course, a beer.

5 garlic cloves
125 ml (4 fl oz/½ cup) extra virgin olive oil
1 kg (2 lb 4 oz) raw prawns (shrimp)
1 tablespoon sea salt
1 teaspoon chilli powder (optional)
lemon wedges, to serve

The only secret to cooking great prawns is to start with really good-quality fresh prawns. Oh, and to share them with good friends.

Salad niçoise

SERVES 2 AS A MAIN

To cook the eggs, put them in a saucepan and add enough cold water to cover. Put on the stove over high heat. As soon as the water comes to the boil set your timer for 4 minutes — this will give you a soft-boiled, runny egg. When the timer goes off remove the eggs and refresh several times in cold water to stop the cooking process and then peel straight away.

Put the potatoes in a saucepan, cover with water and bring to the boil, then cook for 3 minutes or until almost soft, then add the beans and cook for a further 3 minutes, or until the beans and potatoes are tender. Drain and cool under slightly running water.

Assemble the salad in a bowl. You can tear the lettuce into large pieces or leave it whole depending on the size of the leaves and your preference — I do a bit of both. Place the lettuce in a bowl with the halved tomatoes, capers, anchovies and olives along with the still-warm potatoes (halved or whole) and the still warm beans — the residual warmth will help meld all the beautiful flavours together.

Whisk the olive oil and vinegar together for the dressing. Pour the dressing over the salad. Get your hands in the bowl and give it all a good but gentle toss to combine all the ingredients. Again the warmth of the beans and potato really helps release the oil from the anchovy allowing it to melt and combine with the dressing.

Generously season the fish with freshly ground black pepper and a little salt if you want but remember as you have anchovies, olives and capers in the dressing you already have a fair bit of salt. Cook the fish in a hot frying pan or on the barbecue with a splash of olive oil. You should only need to turn the pieces once. If you are using tuna, it should be rare in the middle.

Carefully arrange half the salad on the plate, place 1 sliced tuna steak or 2 nannygai fillets sliced over one side of the salad, then carefully cut the egg in half, place it on top of the salad and allow the yolk to drip out. Repeat with the remaining ingredients.

2 eggs

6–8 small (4 cm/1½ inch long) kipfler (fingerling) potatoes, peeled

150 g (5½ oz) green beans

about 10 nice soft cos (romaine) lettuce leaves from the heart of the lettuce

8 cherry tomatoes, halved

2 teaspoons salted capers, drained and rinsed

8–10 anchovy fillets

16 kalamata olives

3 tablespoons olive oil, plus extra, for pan-frying

3 tablespoons red wine vinegar

2 tuna steaks or 4 nannygai fillets, without skin

Nannygai is a white-fleshed fish native to southern waters of Australia. It is also called bright redfish, red fish and red snapper.

Scallop, squid and venison chorizo salad

SERVES 4

1 red capsicum (pepper)

1 yellow capsicum (pepper)

2 large squid tubes

olive oil

12 scallops

1 chorizo sausage (I used a venison chorizo), thinly sliced

½ iceberg lettuce, roughly torn

1 large handful of baby English spinach leaves

1 large handful of rocket (arugula)

1 fennel bulb, thinly sliced (optional)

3 tablespoons olive oil

2 tablespoons sherry vinegar

To prepare the capsicums, slice the sides from the core so you have four flat sides from each capsicum and place them, skin side up, under a hot grill (broiler). Let them blister and burn until blackened and then place them in a plastic bag to sweat for 5 minutes. Peel the skins off and thinly slice the flesh.

Clean the squid tubes, removing any skin and cartilage. Cut the squid tube on one side so that you can open it out into a square or rectangle. Make sure the inside is clean. Score the soft inside flesh quite deeply to form a diamond pattern. Season with salt and pepper and cook, scored side down, on a hot barbecue plate with a splash of olive oil.

Season the scallops with salt and pepper and add to the barbecue plate to cook. Add the chorizo to the barbecue with a splash of olive oil. Turn the squid and cook the other side and do the same with the scallops and chorizo. The squid will naturally curl up into a roll which you can then cut into 3–4 pieces. When everything is cooked remove to a bowl and keep warm.

Put your salad leaves and fennel in a bowl and mix through about half of the red capsicum and an equal amount of the yellow capsicum. Whisk together the olive oil and sherry vinegar and dress the salad. Tip the seafood and chorizo into the bowl with the salad including any and all of the juices. Give it all a good mix and then carefully arrange on a plate, making sure the seafood and chorizo is distributed equally. Top with some more of the red and yellow capsicum, if you like.

The key to this is fresh, fresh, fresh. Whatever you do, please don't use frozen seafood in the salad. It will be watery and tasteless.

Barramundi moolie

RECIPE BY JIMMY SHU FROM HANUMAN RESTAURANTS, DARWIN AND ALICE SPRINGS

SERVES 2

Heat 3 tablespoons of the oil over medium–high heat in a wok, add half the curry leaves (be careful as the oil might spit) and cook briefly until crisp. Remove with a slotted spoon and set aside. Discard the oil.

Season the barramundi fillets with a pinch of salt, then set aside. Heat the rest of the oil in the wok over medium heat and stir-fry the onion until it softens and the ends start to colour. Add the garlic and continue to stir fry or cook for another 3 minutes. Add the chillies, remaining uncooked curry leaves and tomato. Cook for 1–2 minutes or until the tomato has softened, then add the turmeric, coconut cream and 100 ml (3½ fl oz) water.

Bring to the boil and simmer for 5 minutes, add ½ teaspoon salt and taste to check for seasoning. Gently add the barramundi to the liquid and poach for 7 minutes. Serve immediately with the fried curry leaves.

4 tablespoons vegetable oil
2 curry leaf sprigs, picked
300 g (10½ oz) barramundi fillets,
    cut into 5 cm (2 inch) cubes
¼ red onion, sliced
3 garlic cloves, chopped
4 red bird's eye chillies, bruised
½ tomato, diced
½ teaspoon ground turmeric
400 ml (14½ fl oz) coconut cream

Butter-poached marron

RECIPE BY TONY HOWELL FROM CAPE LODGE, MARGARET RIVER

SERVES 3

3 whole, live marron or lobster
300 ml (10½ fl oz) fish stock
300 g (10½ oz) butter
300 ml (10½ fl oz) dry white wine
2 thyme sprigs
5 peppercorns
3 dill sprigs
1 garlic bulb, halved

PUFF PASTRY DISCS
2 sheets ready-made puff pastry
1 egg
2 tablespoons milk

For the puff pastry discs: Preheat the oven to 200°C (400°F/Gas 6). Cut four 10 cm (4 inch) diameter rounds from the puff pastry sheets. Place on baking trays lined with baking paper. Combine the egg and milk, brush over the pastry and cook for 10–15 minutes, or until puffed and golden. Set aside.

Place the marron in the freezer for about an hour until they are unconscious. Then place them in an Asian steamer basket over a large saucepan of boiling water for 2 minutes. Remove from the heat and cool in an ice bath. Cut in half — the marron is now ready for poaching.

Put all the ingredients, except for the marron, in a saucepan. Bring to a simmer then place the marron in the liquid and simmer for about 2 minutes. Remove the marron from the liquid and serve with a tablespoon of liquid over the top. Serve with steamed greens and a puff pastry disc if desired.

Live marron are available from specialist seafood suppliers and may be substituted with small lobsters.

Salmon with fig and bresaola

RECIPE BY CHRIS TAYLOR FROM FRASER'S RESTAURANT, PERTH

SERVES 3

6 x 60 g (2¼ oz) pieces of Atlantic salmon (belly if possible or thinly sliced fillet ensuring that the fishmonger has scaled the fish before slicing)
1 small bunch watercress, picked
3 figs (Black Genoa if available), each cut into 6 wedges
100 g (3½ oz) Persian feta cheese
24 pieces bresaola (air-dried beef), thinly sliced
juice of 1 lemon
3 tablespoons extra virgin olive oil

Cut small incisions across the flesh side of the belly of the salmon.

Put the watercress, fig wedges and Persian feta in a non-metallic bowl. Tear the bresaola slices into halves and add to the bowl.

Combine the lemon juice and olive oil, then season with salt and pepper and pour half into the bowl, reserving the other half. Toss well to coat the salad. Sear the salmon, presentation side first, on a hot chargrill pan for about 5 seconds, then turn it over and sear for a further 5 seconds.

Divide salad evenly between three plates. Place two pieces of salmon on top of the salad and dress with the reserved lemon olive oil.

Dukkah is an Egyptian speciality of roasted hazelnuts, sesame, coriander and cumin seeds, pistachio nuts, salt and pepper. Most often used for dipping with bread and olive oil, it is also an excellent accompaniment to this dish and can be sprinkled over the salmon just before serving.

Margaret River venison carpaccio with seared Abrolhos scallops

RECIPE BY TONY HOWELL FROM CAPE LODGE, MARGARET RIVER

SERVES 2

Freeze the venison for about 30 minutes to make it easier to slice. Slice the meat as thinly as possible — a meat slicer or a salmon slicing knife will give the best results. Each person should have three paper thin slices.

For the dill mayonnaise: Whisk the eggs, mustard and vinegars together in a small bowl, then slowly whisk in the oil. Season with salt and pepper and whisk in the dill and lemon.

Lay the slices of venison on a cold plate not overlapping, drizzle with olive oil, then sprinkle with capers, shaved parmesan and some freshly ground black pepper. Dress with the dill mayonnaise.

Briefly sear the scallops in a frying pan over very high heat then place on top of the venison and serve immediately.

120 g (4¼ oz) Margaret River venison
    loin, trimmed
olive oil, to taste
baby capers, drained and rinsed, to taste
shaved parmesan cheese, to taste
4 Abrolhos scallops (see note)

DILL MAYONNAISE
2 eggs
½ teaspoon dijon mustard
1 tablespoon white wine vinegar
250 ml (9 fl oz/1 cup) vegetable oil
1–2 tablespoons chopped dill

Abrolhos scallops are Western Australian Southern saucer scallops and are renowned for their sweet flavour and silky texture.

Fruit soup with feta

SERVES 4

Heat the orange juice, sugar and several of the mint leaves in a saucepan over low heat until the sugar is dissolved, then pour into a bowl and sit the bowl in ice or in the freezer to cool.

Remove the flesh from the dragon fruit and watermelon — you should have equal amounts — and blend in a blender until puréed, then pour into a bowl. Chop 1½ tablespoons of mint and add to the fruit purée. Then add the strained chilled orange juice mixture, the Prosecco and the lime juice. Taste and adjust with salt and pepper where necessary.

Ladle into a soup bowl and scatter with finely diced feta. Garnish with a sprig of mint.

juice of 2½ oranges

4 tablespoons caster (superfine) sugar

1 large handful of mint leaves

1 red and 3 white dragon fruit

¼ small watermelon

250 ml (9 fl oz/1 cup) Prosecco (dry Italian sparkling wine)

juice of 1 lime

30 g (1 oz) Greek feta cheese, finely diced (see note)

Use a Greek feta here due to its saltiness and crumbly texture. If you really hate the idea of a fruit soup and even more so a fruit soup with feta cheese in it then this makes a great granita — just chuck it in your ice-cream maker minus the feta and churn it. When it is nice and frozen serve it in a martini glass with a mint leaf on the top.

SOUTH AUSTRALIA

You can always find quality produce in South Australia – from honey and ice cream to geese, sheep, whiting and marron. It's also a great place for a bit of quiet relaxation, a good spot of fishing or, if you want, a bit of sea lion watching.

The first episode we shot in South Australia was in Fleurieu Peninsula, a place I had never heard of. Now normally when you travel around a lot and you hear of a place with a name like this, alarm bells start to ring and you wonder about what you are going to find. The alarm bells ring even louder when you find out you are staying in a town called Goolwa! I was very relieved to find out that Goolwa had a really cool little brew pub called the Steam Exchange Brewery. Unfortunately, we didn't have time to film there but we did get down there for a couple of ales. It turns out that Goolwa is a real family-friendly and funky little town, the kind of place I would love to take my family on holiday. It's also only a short hop, skip and a jump to the beach where you can dig up your own cockles. So if you happen to be in South Australia and go down to the beach in the Fleurieu Peninsula and see a bunch of people holding buckets and doing some kind of a hip-wiggling jig, they'll be doing what is known as the cockle dance. I love cockles and cook them up in a simple wine sauce with pasta. In short I had a great time in the Fleurieu — I mixed my own wine blend, cooked stuffed venison at the fabulous Fino restaurant and visited a farm that was both wonderful and very worrisome.

Mundoo Island Angus Beef, run by Colin Grundy and his wife Sally, is in a beautiful part of the world and their beef is superb. The problem is that their farm sits right on the mouth of the Murray River where it meets the ocean. Because of the drought conditions, salt has started to leach through the specially built barrages put there to stop this from happening. The salt is destroying their drinking water which means the cattle are suffering, the land is being contaminated with salt and the future viability of the farm is at stake. Colin is a fourth-generation farmer and I know he was hoping to pass the farm on to one his sons. Sadly, it may not be there in a year or two. I can't really imagine how tough that must be.

Another great place for a family holiday formed the basis of our second South Australian episode and that is Kangaroo Island. You can stay in the local pub, the local hotel, the local B & B or, if you feel like a bit of luxury, the Southern Ocean Lodge — a 21-suite luxury lodge for the rich and famous.

This is a super simple dish and it is also delicious — the hardest part is to make sure your pasta is cooked at the same time that your cockles are cooked. You don't want your pasta to be cooked first and waiting for the cockles to be done as it will dry out and stick together.
If you can't get cockles you can use clams, pipis, razor clams or even mussels.

Cockle linguine

SERVES 4 AS A MAIN

400 g (14 oz) linguine
olive oil
2 garlic cloves, thinly sliced
4 tablespoons chopped garlic chives
1 red bird's eye chilli, thinly sliced
1 kg (2 lb 4 oz) cockles (see note)
125 ml (4 fl oz/½ cup) good-quality
    dry white wine
3 tablespoons finely chopped flat-leaf
    (Italian) parsley

Bring some well-salted water to the boil and cook the pasta for the recommended time until al dente.

Meanwhile, heat a splash of olive oil in a frying pan that has a lid and gently sauté the garlic until softened, then add the garlic chives and chilli and cook for a few minutes more. Turn up the heat and add the cockles and white wine. Put a lid on the pan and cook for a few minutes, shaking the pan occasionally. Once all the cockles are opened, sprinkle with parsley and keep warm. Discard any cockles that remain tightly closed. Drain the pasta, add to the pan with the cockles and mix well.

Serve the linguine on a large platter with crusty bread and a glass of white wine.

There is nothing more satisfying than going down to the beach with a bucket and digging up a feed of fresh cockles. If you do this, they will need to be purged of sand by soaking them in salted cold water (sea water) for about an hour.

Citrus lamb

RECIPE BY LYN WHEATON FROM STRANRAER LODGE, KANGAROO ISLAND

SERVES 4

2 teaspoons cumin seeds

2 tablespoons rosemary

grated zest of 1 lemon

grated zest of 1 orange

2½ tablespoons extra virgin olive oil

4 x 200 g (7 oz) lamb backstraps or
    loin fillets

Preheat the oven to 200°C (400°F/Gas 6). Pound the cumin and rosemary and some salt and pepper using a mortar and pestle until finely ground. Add the lemon and orange zests and stir in the oil.

Place the mixture in a shallow dish, then take one of the backstraps and roll it through the mixture, making sure to coat the lamb well. Repeat with the remaining backstraps.

Heat a heavy-based frying pan over medium heat, then sear the lamb on both sides, 3–4 minutes in total.

Transfer the lamb to the oven and cook for 6–7 minutes. Set aside and rest for 5 minutes. Serve on a bed of couscous.

When Lyn cooked this dish for me I loved its simplicity and its wonderful, vibrant summer flavour.

Venison stuffed with marinated figs and walnuts

SERVES 2

The night before you want to eat, put the figs in a resealable sandwich bag, then pour in the Madeira, seal tightly and give the bag and contents a bit of a rub and squeeze so that all the figs are well lubricated. Leave in the bag until ready to use.

Preheat the oven to 220°C (425°F/Gas 7). With a sharp knife, cut a tunnel all the way through the middle of the topside. Make the hole as big as you dare but do not cut all the way through or you won't be able to stuff it.

Place the well-marinated figs into a bowl and thoroughly mix through the walnuts, rosemary, parsley and goat's cheese and season with a little salt and pepper. Stuff this mixture into the hole through the centre of the topside and season the outside with salt and pepper. Add a splash of olive oil to an ovenproof frying pan and cook the venison over high heat until sealed and slightly coloured, then transfer to the oven for about 15 minutes for a medium-rare finish. Remove the venison from the pan and keep warm.

Return the pan to the hotplate and deglaze with the extra Madeira and butter to make a rich and luscious sauce.

Slice the topside into 3–4 cm (1¼–1½ inch) thick strips on the diagonal, place three pieces on a plate and drizzle some of the sauce around the plate and over the venison. You could have this with a side of mash or perhaps some roasted potatoes and a side of beans or a salad — it really depends on the time of year and your mood.

185 g (6½ oz/1 cup) chopped dried figs
125 ml (4 fl oz/½ cup) Madeira
500 g venison topside (see note)
75 g (2½ oz/¾ cup) walnuts, chopped
3 tablespoons finely chopped rosemary
3 tablespoons finely chopped flat-leaf (Italian) parsley
150 g (5½ oz) goat's cheese
olive oil
125 ml (4 fl oz/½ cup) Madeira, extra
30 g (1 oz) butter

Cut the topside lengthways down the middle so you have two pieces of equal size about 15–20 cm (6–8 inches) long, and 5–6 cm (2–2½ inches) wide and about 250 g (9 oz) each. You could also use a large backstrap or loin.

Slow-braised goose in cherry beer

SERVES 4

Wash and then pat dry the goose or duck leg quarters, then trim them of excess skin and fat, trying to remove as much fat as possible but not too much skin. Combine the spices and salt and rub the mixture well into each of the leg quarters. Refrigerate overnight — the longer you leave them, the better the flavour will be.

Brown the meat, skin side down, in a hot non-stick frying pan — you will not need any oil as the meat will release plenty. Once the skin is brown and crisp, turn and brown the other side. Remove from the pan. Discard most of the fat from the pan, leaving a couple of tablespoons for cooking the shallots. Cook the shallots for a couple of minutes then add the Kriek Lambic and the chicken stock. Reduce this down by about one-third. Season with salt and pepper.

Preheat the oven to 160°C (315°F/Gas 2–3). Place the goose in an ovenproof dish, preferably a heavy one where it will fit snuggly and then pour over the braising liquid and shallots. Cover with baking paper and a tight-fitting lid and bake for 1½–2 hours. Turn the meat after an hour. Check that the liquid is not bubbling too hard as you just want it to be gently simmering. Once the goose is 'pull apart' tender, carefully lift it out of the liquid and put on a baking tray. Increase the oven temperature to 220°C (425°F/Gas 7) and roast for 6–7 minutes, keeping an eye on it, until the skin becomes crisp.

Place the braising pan with the shallots and cooking liquid on the stove — if there is a lot of fat carefully skim it off. Over a gentle heat add some of the cherry juice — the amount depends on how much liquid is left in the pan but let's say about 125–250 ml (4–9 fl oz/½–1 cup). Also throw in about 100 g (3½ oz/½ cup) of the cherries. Increase the heat and reduce the sauce, all the time scraping the bottom of the pan to get any cooked bits off the pan and into the sauce. Once it is reduced to your liking, check for seasoning and then it is ready.

Serve with polenta and steamed bok choy (pak choy), green beans or braised red cabbage. Drizzle the sauce over the meat and around the plate.

4 goose (or duck) leg quarters
1 teaspoon ground coriander
1 teaspoon dried thyme
½ teaspoon crushed black peppercorns
½ teaspoon allspice
¼ teaspoon garlic powder
1 teaspoon salt
8 French shallots, peeled and cut into thirds
375 ml (13 fl oz) bottle of Kriek Lambic (see note)
250 ml (9 fl oz/1 cup) chicken stock
700 g (1 lb 9 oz) jar of pitted morello cherries

Lambic is a Belgian beer. Once the beer has finished fermenting, sour cherries are added and the beer undergoes a second fermentation. The cherries add colour, some sweetness and also a sourness that makes the beer quite complex and delicious. It comes in small bottles similar to Champagne, complete with a cork. Other flavours include framboise (raspberry), cassis (blackcurrant) and peach.

King George whiting with a white wine butter and caper sauce

SERVES 2

plain (all-purpose) flour, for coating
2 whole King George whiting,
    cleaned and gutted
100 g (3½ oz) butter
½ lemon
125 ml (4 fl oz/½ cup) dry white wine
2 tablespoons salted capers, drained
    and rinsed
8 baby carrots, peeled
8 asparagus spears, trimmed
1 tablespoon ligurian or other honey
lemon wedges, to serve

Season the flour with salt and pepper, dredge the fish through and then dust off any excess. Heat half of the butter in a large non-stick frying pan over medium heat and, when foaming, add the fish. When the skin is lightly browned, turn the fish over, give them a generous squeeze of lemon and cook the other side. Remove the fish from the pan and keep warm.

Deglaze the pan with white wine, scatter in the capers and then add the remaining butter. Gently cook down until all the flavours are combined.

Blanch or steam the carrots and asparagus, drain and return to the pot. Drizzle over some of the honey and then toss together allowing some of the steaming liquid to loosen the honey and coat the vegetables.

Stack the carrots and asparagus on one half of the plate then place the whiting beside them. Spoon some of the caper sauce over the whiting. Garnish with wedges of lemon.

This is my wife Andrea's recipe. I stole it from her as she's a really good cook!

Venison carpaccio

RECIPE BY DAVID SWAIN FROM FINO RESTAURANT, WILLUNGA

SERVES 4 AS A STARTER

200 g (7 oz) venison loin, trimmed
1 small fresh horseradish root, peeled
zest of 1 small lemon
2 tablespoons crème fraîche
small handful of watercress, to garnish
extra virgin olive oil, for drizzling

Cut the venison into eight thin slices. Place a slice between two sheets of plastic wrap and lightly flatten with the side of a meat mallet until paper-thin. Put aside and repeat with the other slices.

For the horseradish cream, grate the horseradish and lemon zest as finely as possible and place in a bowl. Juice the lemon and add to the horseradish and lemon zest, then fold in the crème fraîche and season with salt and pepper.

Place two slices of venison on each plate. Divide the horseradish cream between the plates, then garnish with watercress, drizzle with olive oil and season with salt and pepper.

Fino is a great little restaurant but it is missing something — a menu! David cooks up a selection of wonderful dishes based on local produce and he also has a herb garden that not only meets the restaurant's needs, but also provides a gorgeous environment for the diners.

King crab salad

RECIPE BY TIM BOURKE FROM SOUTHERN OCEAN LODGE, KANGAROO ISLAND

SERVES 6

If you are starting with fresh crab — put the crab in the freezer for about an hour until it is unconscious. Remove the top shell by lifting the flap on the underside. Remove the gills (the spongey grey fingers) and any muck by rinsing very lightly and quickly under running water.

Using a cleaver, cut the crab into four pieces and, using the back of a cleaver or knife, gently crack open the claws. Steam for 5–10 minutes, depending upon the size of the crab, until the crabmeat is just cooked.

Once the crab has cooled, remove the crabmeat. Segment the grapefruit, reserving the juice. Finely chop the mint. Combine 300 g of crabmeat with the mint, olive oil and some of the grapefruit juice to taste. Season with sea salt.

Mix the avocado with the shallot and chilli, a drizzle of olive oil and sea salt. Using an egg ring (to help give that lovely, formal tower shape) place one-sixth of the avocado mix into the ring, top with one-sixth of the crab mix, two grapefruit segments then remove ring and garnish with mini lettuce leaves and baby coriander. Repeat with remaining ingredients.

1 live king crab or 300 g (10½ oz)
    fresh crabmeat
1 ruby grapefruit
4 mint sprigs, picked
50 ml (1½ fl oz) olive oil
1 avocado, flesh removed and chopped
½ French shallot, finely chopped
1 long red chilli, seeded and
    finely chopped
mini lettuce mix or sprouts, to garnish
baby coriander, to garnish

VICTORIA

Try this experiment: get a map of Victoria, close your eyes and jab your index finger on a spot. I guarantee if you travel to that location you will find great produce, good food and, of course, fantastic scenery and people.

Living in Melbourne means that I can jump on my motorbike and within an hour or so, I can cruise around the Mornington Peninsula for the best chocolates in Australia, stop at Foxeys Hangout for lunch, eat locally produced beef and veggies while sipping on wine made from the grapes that are grown just outside the restaurant windows. Or I can pop into Red Hill Brewery for a beer matched to some Red Hill Cheese.

Head up to Bright in north-east Victoria and you can spend the day picking your own apples, hazelnuts and olives and afterwards pop into Milawa free-range chooks and get a chicken so you can whip up a chicken casserole at home. Or just go to Simone's Restaurant to get excellent home-style Italian food.

On your journey around Victoria, you might stop at the Yarra Valley, Healesville and dine at Giant Steps Winery. They make their own bread, wine and roast their own coffee (they also recently installed a brewery). You could go to the Mont De Lancey food markets and pick up some great locally made chutneys, jams, sausages, free-range organic pork and then relax at Chris Helleren's restaurant and enjoy her rabbit fricassee.

And there is more on offer. There is the Bellarine Peninsula with its mussel and abalone farm, hydroponic tomatoes, strawberries, sheep you don't have to shear, fresh seafood, juicy blueberries, fabulous goat's cheese, bread baked in an original 150-year-old oven and of course, Bellarine Estate wines and beers.

If you still have petrol in your tank, then head out to Gippsland; the scenery is magical and the produce even better. Get yourself out on the Gippsland Lakes and try your hand at either catching some eel or purchasing smoked eel from Bryn and Peter at East Coast Eels. Australia's largest producer of asparagus is here along with some of the best organic lamb grown anywhere in the world! As for the bountiful array of fresh fish coming in, well what can I say? I was going to go out on John's fishing boat, duly arrived at the wharf at 4.30 am ready to sail, got on the boat and it promptly broke down. It was a rather cold four hours waiting for the other boats to come in but I made up for it by using some of the fresh fish off the boat to cook up a bouillabaisse on the wharf for all the fishermen.

Yep, get a map of Victoria and take a magical food tour around this great state.

Red Hill Brewery steak sandwich

RECIPE BY DAVID SIMMS FROM THE RED HILL BREWERY CAFÉ

SERVES 4

Marinate the steak in the ale, garlic, rosemary and thyme for at least 2 hours, preferably overnight.

Caramelise the onions by frying slowly in a splash of oil over low–medium heat until golden brown. Pan-fry the bacon to your liking.

In a very hot frying pan, add a splash of oil and heat. Add the steak and sear 3 minutes, turn over and cook for another 3 minutes, topping with some onion and cheese during cooking until the cheese melts.

While the steak is cooking, chargrill the bread. Spread one side of the bread with chutney, top with lettuce, tomato and bacon, then add the steak with cheese and onion and the other piece of bread. Serve with a baked potato or wedges.

2 porterhouse steaks (about 300 g/ 10½ oz each), cut horizontally to create four steaks

2 x 330 ml (11¼ fl oz) bottles Red Hill Brewery Scotch Ale or other dark ale

2 garlic cloves, crushed

1 sprig rosemary

1 sprig thyme

2 large onions, sliced

olive oil

4 bacon slices

200 g (7 oz) cheddar cheese, sliced

8 slices wood-fired sourdough

Brewhouse Larder Range tomato chutney or other good-quality chutney

lettuce

2 tomatoes, sliced

The scotch ale is perfect as a marinade or as an accompaniment to the steak. Its caramel sweetness and roasted malt character matches well with the caramelised onion.

This mixture is enough for 10 mussels. If you want to make more, simply increase the ingredients accordingly, allowing 10 mussels per person.

Barbecued mussels with garlic parsley lemon butter

SERVES 1

25 g (1 oz) butter
1 garlic clove, crushed
juice of ½ lemon
1 tablespoon chopped flat-leaf
    (Italian) parsley
10 mussels

Melt the butter in a small saucepan, then add the garlic, lemon juice and parsley — give it a good mix and it's ready.

Preheat your barbecue to high. Scrub the mussels and pull out the hairy beards. Discard any broken mussels, or open ones that don't close when tapped on the work surface. Rinse well. Place the mussels over the flames and let them cook until they open. Once they open, spoon some of the butter mixture into each mussel so that it cooks in all those lovely flavours. You may need to assist your mussels to open wide enough which is fine but do not force any open that remain tightly shut — throw them out.

Keep an eye on the heat of the barbecue — you want your mussels to open but sometimes it can get too hot and burn the shell. Also, if your mussels are really fresh they will still have seawater in them. This will do two things — provide enough salt so you won't need to add salt to the butter mix and steam the mussel inside before it opens. Be careful when taking the mussels off the barbecue as you don't want to spill all of the delicious juice your mussel has been cooked in.

The best way to eat them is to carefully pry off one side of the mussel shell and then use the shell with the mussel sitting in it like a spoon — eat and make loud slurping noises!

You can use black or green-lipped mussels for this dish. I was lucky enough to get them straight out of Port Phillip Bay where they grow black mussels. Try to buy large mussels as they will not only be easier to cook but easier to add the butter.

Salt-baked snapper

RECIPE BY SIMON FAWCETT FROM BELLARINE ESTATE, PORTARLINGTON

SERVES 4

Preheat oven to 180°C (350°F/Gas 4). Coat the snapper with olive oil.

Whisk the egg whites until soft peaks form, then fold in the salt. Coat the fish in the salt mix, place on baking tray and bake for 45 minutes. Once cooked, slowly remove the salt mix and place the snapper onto a serving platter.

For the salad: Mix all ingredients together and season with salt, pepper, olive oil and a squeeze of lemon. Serve on the plate next to the fish add a lemon wedge and enjoy.

1 large snapper, about 2kg (4 lb 8 oz)
olive oil
4 egg whites
1 kg (2 lb 4 oz) rock salt
lemon wedges

SALAD
300 g (10½ oz) rocket (arugula)
12 blanched asparagus spears
150 g (5½ oz) Drysdale goat's cheese
30 ml (1 fl oz) olive oil
squeeze of lemon juice

There are many recipes for raspberry vinaigrette; this is one I use — if you are not in the mood to make your own vinaigrette, then just buy a bottle.

Fig and goat's cheese salad

RECIPE BY NIGEL PITMAN FROM THE OL' DUKE, PORTARLINGTON

SERVES 4

6 ripe figs
200 g (7 oz) Drysdale goat's cheese chèvre
150 g (5½ oz/4¼ cups) wild
    rocket (arugula)
½ red onion, thinly sliced
100 g (3½ oz/1 cup) walnuts

RASPBERRY VINAIGRETTE
30 g (1 oz/¼ cup) frozen raspberries
3 tablespoons white wine vinegar
3 tablespoons extra virgin olive oil
½ teaspoon soft brown sugar
1 teaspoon dijon mustard
1 small garlic clove, crushed

Cut the figs into wedges and chop up the chèvre. Toss all the salad ingredients together in a bowl.

For the vinaigrette: Combine the raspberries and vinegar in a saucepan over medium heat. Simmer for 5 minutes. Remove from the heat and allow to cool, then strain the raspberries, reserving the liquid. Combine 3 tablespoons of the raspberry vinegar, the olive oil, sugar, mustard, garlic, salt and freshly ground black pepper in a jar, put the lid on and give it a good shake to combine.

Dress the salad with the vinaigrette, then serve.

If you like, you can finish the salad with a scattering of some crispy prosciutto pieces.

Smoked eel dip

SERVES 4 AS A STARTER

115 g (4 oz) smoked eel meat, skin
   removed (see note)
3 teaspoons cream cheese
3 teaspoons sour cream
1 teaspoon cream
2 teaspoons prepared horseradish
   (not creamed)
2½ teaspoons lemon juice
½ teaspoon chopped dill, plus extra,
   to garnish
toasted sourdough, to serve

Put the eel in a blender and pulse to break up the meat, then add all the other ingredients and blend to a smooth paste. Season with salt and pepper, then blend again before turning it out into a serving bowl. Garnish with a little more chopped dill and serve the dip with thin slices of toasted sourdough.

You can buy smoked eel meat from specialist fishmongers or the fish market. If you don't like the idea of eel, you can use smoked trout instead.

Moroccan spiced lamb stuffed with medjool dates and Drysdale fettina and a tagine of sweet potato

RECIPE BY GRAHAM HENDERSON FROM BELLARINE ESTATE   SERVES 4

Trim the lamb and remove any excess fat, keeping the skin attached but peel it back from meat.

Mix the dates and fettina and spread half over each loin. Roll the skin back to cover the meat and secure tightly with kitchen string tied at 2.5 cm (1 inch) intervals all the way along. Grind all the dried spices together using a mortar and pestle and rub all over the lamb.

Pour a splash of olive oil into a frying pan and heat the pan until hot. Sear the lamb all over until all the fat is rendered and the skin is crisp and golden brown, then season liberally with fine sea salt.

For the tagine: Gently fry the sweet potato in a splash of oil, without allowing it to brown. After a few minutes add the shallots and continue cooking for a couple of minutes, then add the garlic, chilli and rosemary. Add the tomato and bring to a simmer, then add the stock and bring back to a simmer. Transfer the mixture to a casserole dish with a lid or a tagine and sit the lamb on top of the tagine. 'Pot roast' the dish with a lid for about 40 minutes if you want it pink.

To prepare the capers, put them and the oil in a saucepan over medium heat and heat until the capers start to turn golden. Lift out the capers with a slotted spoon and drain on paper towel.

After roasting, remove the lamb, cover loosely with foil and leave to rest for about 15 minutes before carving.

Add the preserved lemon to the tagine and taste before seasoning — the preserved lemon can negate the need for much salt. Arrange the carved lamb on top of the tagine and garnish with the almonds, fried capers and sprigs of coriander.

LAMB

2 x 500 g (1 lb 2 oz) boned lamb loins, with all the skin and fat attached
150 g (5½ oz) fresh medjool dates, pitted and chopped
150 g (5½ oz) Drysdale goat's fettina, or your favourite feta cheese
½ cinnamon stick
6 juniper berries
4 cloves
4 black peppercorns
olive oil

TAGINE

1 kg (2 lb 4 oz) orange sweet potato, diced
olive oil
2 French shallots, finely chopped
2 garlic cloves, finely chopped
1 bird's eye chilli, finely chopped
1 rosemary sprig, chopped
400 g (14 oz) tin of chopped tomatoes
500 ml (17 fl oz/2 cups) chicken stock
zest of 1 preserved lemon, finely chopped

GARNISH

2 tablespoons salted capers, drained and rinsed
250 ml (9 fl oz/1 cup) vegetable oil
flaked almonds, toasted
coriander (cilantro) sprigs

When I cooked this recipe I was lucky enough to have organic pork chops and wonderful organic vegetables from Heronswood Gardens on the Mornington Peninsula.

Barbecued pork chops with barbecued vegetable salad

SERVES 4

For the marinade: Put all the spices in a bowl, mix them all up and then add a splash of beer and the sesame oil and mix again. Dip your finger into the mix and taste it: if you like it, good; if not, work out why and adjust the proportions accordingly.

Either using a mortar and pestle or on your chopping board, smash your peeled garlic with some salt until it is like a paste and then slather this all over the meat. Place the meat into the marinade and make sure the chops are well coated. Set aside while you prepare the vegetable salad.

For the salad: Rub the beetroot, turnips, garlic, carrots and spring onions with half the olive oil and season with salt. Wrap the beetroot, turnips and garlic individually in foil and place on a hot barbecue with a heatproof bowl over them to keep the heat in. Leave them for about 15 minutes or until cooked. Chargrill the carrots and spring onions on the barbecue until they are cooked and nicely coloured.

When the beetroot and turnips are cooked, remove them from the foil, carefully peel then cut in half and place them in a large salad bowl. Add the carrots, spring onions and goat's cheese to the bowl and squeeze the cooked bulb of garlic so that all of the yummy mushy garlic cloves fall into the salad. Dress with the remaining olive oil and red wine vinegar and toss it all together.

Barbecue the pork chops until cooked about 5–7 minutes each side, or until cooked to your liking.

Put your pork chop on a plate, add a nice portion of salad on the side, garnish with some chives and enjoy!

4 garlic cloves, peeled
4 pork chops

MARINADE
½ teaspoon ground cumin
½ teaspoon ground coriander
½ teaspoon chilli powder
1 teaspoon onion powder
½ teaspoon salt
1 teaspoon pepper
2 teaspoons sichuan pepper, ground using a mortar and pestle
160 ml (5¼ fl oz) dark ale
1 teaspoon sesame oil

SALAD
4 baby beetroot (beets)
4 baby turnips
1 garlic bulb
8 baby carrots
1 bunch of bulb spring onions (scallions)
4 tablespoons olive oil
80 g (2¾ oz) goat's cheese, crumbled
1 tablespoon red wine vinegar
snipped chives, to garnish

Thai beef salad

SERVES 2 AS A MAIN OR 4 AS A STARTER

2 x 250g (9 oz) porterhouse steaks

2 garlic cloves

2 cm (¾ inch) piece of fresh ginger, grated

1 bunch of mint

3 tablespoons soy sauce

150 g (5½ oz) glass noodles (very fine rice noodles)

1 bunch of coriander (cilantro) with roots

2 small red chillies, chopped

juice of 2–3 limes

3 tablespoons fish sauce

2–3 tablespoons grated palm sugar (jaggery)

1 carrot, peeled and julienned

1 cucumber, peeled, seeded and julienned

½ red onion, thinly sliced

1 handful bean sprouts, trimmed

150 g (5½ oz) enoki mushrooms, trimmed

1 butter lettuce

1 mignonette lettuce

peanut oil

crushed peanuts, to garnish

Trim all the fat off the steak and put into a bowl. Add 1 crushed garlic clove, the ginger, 6 finely chopped mint leaves, the soy sauce and season with salt and pepper. Give it a good mix and let the steak marinate while you make the dressing and salad.

Place the noodles into a bowl, pour over boiling water and stand for 3 minutes or until soft, drain, rinse under cold water and drain again.

To make the dressing, put 3–4 scraped coriander roots in a mortar. Add the remaining clove of garlic and pound these into a paste, adding a little more salt if needed. Add the chillies and pound until it is incorporated into the coriander and garlic. Add the lime juice, fish sauce and palm sugar. Give it all a good grind and, if necessary, pour the dressing into a heatproof bowl and hold it over a gentle flame to warm through and help melt the palm sugar into the mixture. The key to a Thai dressing is the balance between hot (chilli), salty (fish sauce), sour (lime juice) and sweet (palm sugar). As we all have our own individual palate you may need to adjust these measures to suit your own palate, so taste and explore. The first time I made this I didn't sweeten it nearly enough and it was all sour and salt!

For the salad: In a bowl, combine the carrot, cucumber, onion, bean sprouts, mushrooms, a handful of finely chopped coriander leaves, 6 or so roughly torn leaves from each of the lettuces, a handful of roughly torn mint leaves and the glass noodles. Mix so everything is combined and then spoon over half the dressing and mix again.

Fry the steak in a frying pan in a little peanut oil over high heat for 3 minutes each side for medium-rare, or until cooked to your liking. Let the steak rest for a few minutes and then slice thinly.

Take a nice handful of salad and place in the middle of a plate, arrange some meat slices on top and spoon over the rest of the dressing, then scatter with some crushed peanuts to serve.

Make sure you reserve the left-over lettuce for another day. Alternatively, you could use a salad mix or just one style of lettuce. I used two types for the flavour and colour they added to the dish.

This amount of marinade is good for a couple of lamb racks. For a whole boned leg of lamb you will probably want to double the ingredients. Alternatively, you could use lamb backstraps or loin fillets, cut into 10 cm (4 inch) lengths.

Greek-style lamb on the barbecue

SERVES 4

2 x lamb racks, 8–10 points each

MARINADE
3 tablespoons olive oil
3 tablespoons lemon juice
1½ teaspoons chopped oregano
    or marjoram
1½ teaspoons chopped rosemary
1 teaspoon raw (demerara) sugar
½ teaspoon paprika
1 teaspoon tomato paste
    (concentrated purée)
2 garlic cloves, crushed
3 tablespoons red wine
10 g (¼ oz) feta cheese

Combine the marinade ingredients and mix until well incorporated. Taste and adjust accordingly.

Put the lamb racks in a large resealable plastic bag, pour in the marinade and seal the bag. Give it a good rub, massaging the meat in the bag so that the marinade gets into all of the nooks and crannies. Refrigerate for 1–3 days to intensify the marinade flavours.

Cook on the barbecue over direct heat until the meat is cooked to your liking — I like it done a little more than medium. Serve with Greek salad (see opposite page).

Greek salad

Wash the lettuce and then dry it in a salad spinner or with a clean tea towel (dish towel) and put in a salad bowl. Peel the skin off the cucumber, cut in half lengthways and then cut across the cucumber to make small half moons — toss into the salad bowl. Cut the tomatoes in half and then slice each half into six wedges and add to the salad. Scatter the onion over the salad. Throw in the olives and then cut the feta into small cubes and scatter over the salad. Mix everything together.

Mix the oil and vinegars in a jar, add the garlic, mustard and some salt and pepper then put the lid on the jar and give it a good shake. Taste for seasoning and a good balance between the oil, vinegar, garlic and mustard. Pour the dressing over the salad and then give it a good toss to mix through.

300 g (10½ oz) mixed lettuce, leaves
1–2 Lebanese (short) cucumbers
3 large tomatoes
1 red onion, thinly sliced
about 24 kalamata olives
150 g (5½ oz) Greek feta cheese

DRESSING
4 tablespoons olive oil
2 tablespoons balsamic vinegar
2 tablespoons red wine vinegar
1 garlic clove, crushed
1 teaspoon wholegrain mustard

This is one of those meals that you have at least once a month and never tire of. Simple quality ingredients, minimum effort but maximum flavour and enjoyment.

Haloumi is quite a salty cheese so you shouldn't need to season the flour with any salt, however, taste the cheese first to see if it is salty enough for you but remember that cooking the cheese tends to accentuate the saltiness even more.

Smoky spiced haloumi

SERVES 2 AS A STARTER

1 handful plain (all-purpose) flour
about 1 tablespoon smoky tomatina
    spice mix (see note)
250 g (9 oz) haloumi cheese
olive oil
lemon wedges, to serve
mixed salad leaves, to serve

Throw the flour into a resealable plastic bag, add the spice mix and give it a good shake to mix the flour and the spices together.

Cut the haloumi into 3–5 mm (⅛–¼ inch) thick pieces (or to your liking) then toss into the flour. Give the bag a good shake making sure the haloumi is well coated — the cheese should come out orange from the spice mix.

Heat a splash of olive oil in a frying pan or put some oil on your barbecue hotplate. Give the haloumi a bit of a shake to get rid of the excess flour and then put it into the frying pan or on the barbecue and cook. Turn when the haloumi is nicely coloured and cook the other side until coloured and crisp, all up about 2–3 minutes depending on how hot your cooker is.

Serve on a plate with a wedge of lemon and a green salad.

The smoky tomatina is made by a company called Screaming Seeds and is a wonderful mix of spice, smoke, salt and sweetness; in fact all of the blends from the Screaming Seeds Company are terrific so give them a try. You can order off their website if you can't find them at your local gourmet deli: www.screamingseeds.com.au, or you could just use some smoked paprika and garlic powder instead.

Peninsula beef with salsa verde, and grilled asparagus with blood orange

RECIPE BY TONY LEE FROM FOXEYS HANGOUT, MORNINGTON PENINSULA

SERVES 2

Preheat a barbecue or cast-iron chargrill pan to high. For the salsa verde: Put the herbs (leaves only, not the stems) in a food processor with the capers, anchovy, lemon juice and olive oil. Blitz until the leaves are chopped and you have a vibrant green sauce. (If you don't have a food processor, you can chop and mix by hand — the herbs shouldn't be puréed.)

Cut any large bits of fat away from beef. Season with salt and pepper and smear each side of the steaks with vegetable oil before cooking on the barbecue or chargrill pan for 3–5 minutes on each side, or until just cooked to rare or medium–rare. Set aside in a warm place (an oven set to its lowest setting is good) for 5 minutes to rest — this step is very important.

For the asparagus: Preheat a barbecue or cast-iron chargrill pan to hot. Brush the asparagus spears with vegetable oil and cook for about 3 minutes until just tender, turning once.

Place the asparagus on two warm plates with the orange segments, then top with the goat's curd. Sprinkle with the reserved orange juice, a drizzle of extra olive oil, a little salt and pepper and the mint leaves.

Slice the steak on the diagonal and spoon over the salsa verde.

2 x 200 g (7 oz) porterhouse, scotch fillet, rump or eye fillet steaks
vegetable oil
1 bunch of asparagus
1 blood orange, segmented, juices reserved from cutting up the orange
1 tablespoon goat's curd, crumbled
extra virgin olive oil
1 small handful of mint leaves

SALSA VERDE
2 large handfuls of leafy herbs such as basil, flat-leaf (Italian) parsley, mint or rocket (arugula)
2 teaspoons salted capers, drained and rinsed
1 anchovy fillet
juice of 1 lemon
1 tablespoon extra virgin olive oil

I used rice flour in this recipe to give the fish a slightly crispy texture, however, I am not sure that it makes much difference when cooking on a barbecue. I had quite a bit of the seasoned flour left over and we also had some flathead tails so I put the flour into a bowl, poured in some of the Bellarine Bitter and made a beer batter. I dipped the flathead tails into the batter and deep-fried them — they were magnificent! The rice flour crisped them up beautifully and the salty spiciness from the sichuan was really accentuated — in short — it is a great beer batter.

King George whiting on the barbie

SERVES 4 AS A MAIN

1 tablespoon sichuan peppercorns
90 g (3¼ oz/½ cup) rice flour
1 tablespoon sea salt
¼ teaspoon white pepper
10 King George whiting fillets
    (or snapper or bream), skin off
lemon wedges, to serve

Preheat a barbecue plate to high. Put the sichuan peppercorns in a small frying pan and place over high heat on the barbecue and toast gently until they begin to smell fragrant and smoky. Use a mortar and pestle to grind them to a powder.

Place the rice flour, salt, white pepper and sichuan pepper in a plastic bag and shake well to mix the seasoning through the flour. Put the whiting fillets into the bag and give it a good shake, coating the fillets completely.

Oil the hot barbecue plate, remove the whiting fillets from the bag and slap or shake off the excess flour. Place the whiting onto the barbecue plate and cook for several minutes before turning and cooking the other side for several minutes more. The fish should be nicely coloured and flake apart when tested with a fork. Put onto a serving plate and garnish with lemon wedges.

Chinese mussels

RECIPE BY NIGEL PITMAN FROM THE OL' DUKE, PORTARLINGTON

SERVES 4-6 AS A STARTER

Combine the soy sauce, kecap manis, vinegar, spring onions, ginger, coriander and sesame oil in a bowl.

Scrub the mussels and pull out the hairy beards. Discard any broken mussels, or open ones that don't close when tapped on the work surface. Rinse well. To cook the mussels, heat a wide pan or wok over high heat. Add the mussels and shake the pan, then cover with a lid. As the mussels cook and open remove them from the pan and place in a serving bowl. Pour out the mussel juice as it will make the dish too salty. Discard any mussels that remain tightly closed. Pour the sauce into the pan and warm, then pour over the mussels. Top with the tomato and bean sprouts.

100 ml (3½ fl oz) light soy sauce
4 tablespoons kecap manis
4 tablespoons malt vinegar
2 spring onions (scallions), thinly sliced
2 cm (¾ inch) piece of fresh ginger, diced, zested or grated
1 handful of coriander (cilantro) leaves
1 teaspoon sesame oil
2.5 kg (5 lb 8 oz) mussels
2 tomatoes, diced
200 g (7 oz) bean sprouts, trimmed

Home-smoked trout frittata

SERVES 6

For the smoked trout: Mix the salt, sugar, beer, honey and water to make a brine. Mix until the sugar has dissolved. Soak the trout fillets with the skin on for 15–20 minutes. Remove from the brine and pat dry before putting in your smoker or on the barbecue.

To smoke the trout, use small pieces of wood and put them on a triple layer of foil. Then lay that foil directly onto the barbecue burner by removing the cooking grate that sits above it. Place the fish on the grill next to the smoking wood or on a wire rack so that the smoke can surround and envelope the fish — do not put the fish over the wood or too near the flame. Put the lid down and let the smoke do its job. You want the internal temperature of the barbecue to be around 100°C (200°F) and you want a good, constant stream of smoke. Have a spray bottle handy to dampen the flame in case any of the wood catches fire as it will be acrid and make the fish taste unpleasant.

Smoke the trout in the barbecue for 10–15 minutes until the fish flakes when tested with a fork. When the trout is cooked, remove from the barbecue and flake the fish off the skin and discard it.

For the frittata: Beat the eggs with the milk and season with the chilli, cumin and some salt and pepper and set aside.

Cook the potatoes in a splash of olive oil in a hot frying pan for about 15–20 minutes or until cooked and coloured. Set aside.

Put the butter in a hot frying pan and, when foaming, add the red onion and spring onion and cook until softened. Add the dandelion leaves, kale and snow peas and cook until softened, then add the milk and egg mixture. Crumble the smoked trout evenly around the pan and do the same with the feta. Do not stir. Reduce the heat so that the bottom will cook and set but not burn. When the egg is fairly set you can put the pan under the grill (broiler) to cook the top and give it some good colour.

Serve straight from the pan with some bread.

10 bantam eggs or 6 large free-range eggs
125 ml (4 fl oz/½ cup) milk
¼ teaspoon chilli powder
¼ teaspoon ground cumin
6 purple Congo potatoes, peeled and diced
olive oil
25 g (1 oz) butter
½ red onion, thinly sliced
3 spring onions (scallions), thinly sliced
about 50 g (1¾ oz) finely chopped dandelion leaves or rocket (arugula)
about 60 g (2¼ oz) finely chopped kale or silverbeet (Swiss chard)
100 g (3½ oz) snow peas (mangetout), sliced
200 g (7 oz) smoked trout (about 4 fillets, see below)
60 g (2¼ oz) Greek feta cheese

SMOKED TROUT
240 g (8½ oz) salt
95 g (3¼ oz/½ cup) soft brown sugar
125 ml (4 fl oz/½ cup) Rogers' Ale from Little Creatures Brewing company
2 tablespoons honey
2 litres (70 fl oz/8 cups) water
4 rainbow trout fillets, skin on
Hickory or Mesquite woodchips, for smoking

Japanese-style abalone salad on pickled cucumber

SERVES 4 AS A STARTER

1 large fresh abalone
2 teaspoons sesame oil
1 handful of bean sprouts, trimmed
150 g (5½ oz) oyster mushrooms,
   thinly sliced
1 teaspoon sesame seeds, toasted

PICKLED CUCUMBER
1 Lebanese (short) cucumber
3 tablespoons vinegar
1½ tablespoons sugar
1 teaspoon grated fresh ginger

DRESSING
3 tablespoons rice wine
2 tablespoons soy sauce
1 tablespoon sugar
2 teaspoons mirin
about ½ teaspoon fish sauce, to taste

To clean the abalone, place a thin fillet knife against the inside of the portion of the shell and move it inward cutting the muscle attachment close to the shell. Carefully remove the meat from the abalone shell. Trim the head, gills and viscera.

For the pickled cucumber: Peel the cucumber and cut the flesh into long, thin strips or ribbons, discarding the seeds. Put the strips into a colander and sprinkle with 1 teaspoon salt and let sit for 10–15 minutes. Mix the vinegar, sugar and ginger together in a bowl. Rinse and drain the cucumber and put it in the vinegar mixture, then mix and set it aside.

For the dressing: Combine the rice wine, soy sauce, sugar, mirin, fish sauce and ¼ teaspoon salt, then mix well.

Cover the cleaned abalone muscle with plastic wrap and then give it a couple of good whacks with a rolling pin or other heavy blunt object — this will tenderise the meat. Slice the abalone very thinly across the top of the meat. Toss the sliced abalone in a little sesame oil and then flash-fry in a hot pan, turning only once — you should only cook it for 30 seconds to 1 minute; any longer and it will turn into boot leather.

Put a mound of pickled cucumber ribbons on a plate, top with some bean sprouts and then some mushrooms. Place a few slices of abalone on top. Drizzle with the dressing and sprinkle some toasted sesame seeds over the top.

Saffron risotto

RECIPE BY PATRIZIA SIMONE FROM SIMONE'S, BRIGHT

SERVES 4

1 litre (35 fl oz/4 cups) chicken or
   vegetable stock
4 saffron threads
1 onion, finely chopped
3 tablespoons olive oil
1 tablespoon butter
440 g (15½ oz/2 cups) arborio rice
4 tablespoons grated parmesan cheese
3 tablespoons flat-leaf (Italian)
   parsley chopped

Pour the stock into a saucepan with the saffron and bring to a simmer. Always keep it simmering so when you add it to the risotto it doesn't cool the risotto down and make it gluggy.

Sauté the onion in the oil and butter until transparent. Don't brown the onion otherwise this will impart bitterness. Add the rice to the pan, stir to coat for about 2–3 minutes.

Add some stock to the rice, half a ladle at a time while continuously stirring, allowing the stock to be absorbed by the rice before adding the next ladleful. If the stock is added too quickly or the risotto is not stirred regularly it will not develop the creamy texture which it is famous for. Keep adding stock until the rice is cooked. The rice will still be slightly firm to the bite (al dente). Remove the pan from the heat, add the parmesan and parsley and serve immediately.

Don't ever wash rice for risotto — you will just wash away the starch which helps give risotto its creamy texture.

Beer scrambled eggs with smoked trout and goat's cheese toast

SERVES 2

Preheat the oven to 200°C (400°F/Gas 6). Lightly coat the tomatoes with some olive oil, being careful not to pull them off the vine. Put them in a roasting tin and put them in the oven until they have broken down, or about 10–15 minutes.

Break the eggs into a bowl, whisk together, then add the cream and beer. Give it another good whisk, add the dill and some salt and pepper, and whisk again.

Put the butter into a warm frying pan over low–medium heat and let it melt; when it begins to foam tip in your egg mix. Let the eggs cook gently, folding them every few minutes. When you think they are almost cooked, fold through the trout so it is mixed through and then remove the pan from heat. The idea is to remove the pan from the heat before the eggs are fully cooked as they will continue to cook once removed.

Serve the eggs on a plate with the tomatoes still on the vine. Lightly toast the bread and place the goat's cheese over it, cut into strips and serve on the side of the plate.

8 cherry tomatoes on the vine

olive oil

4 free-range eggs

3 tablespoons cream

3 tablespoons Little Creatures Pale Ale or other light ale

2 teaspoons finely chopped fresh dill

30 g (1 oz) butter

150 g (5½ oz) smoked trout fillet (see recipe, page 135), flaked and any bones removed

2 slices of sourdough bread, thinly sliced

75 g (2½ oz) good-quality soft goat's cheese

It can be fiddly buying a whole rabbit, cutting it down and removing all the meat but it's worth it. However, I guess if you really didn't want to do that you could joint the rabbit, and cook it with the pork as described. Once cooked, pull all the tender meat off the bones. Be aware that it may take longer to cook this way.

Pork and rabbit rillettes

SERVES 6 AS A STARTER

Preheat the oven to 160°C (315°F/Gas 2–3). Cut the pork neck and belly and rabbit into 1 cm (½ inch) cubes and mix with the salt, coating everything well. Using kitchen string tie together the bay leaves and rosemary, then wrap in muslin (cheesecloth) with the juniper berries, cloves and peppercorns and tie to make a bouquet garni. Place the meat, bouquet garni and beer in a casserole dish, mix everything together, put the lid on and cook in the oven for 3 hours, or until the meat is tender and falling apart.

Meanwhile, render down the pork fat by slowly cooking it over low heat in a heavy-based deep saucepan. Strain any solids from it and reserve the liquid.

Remove the bouquet garni from the casserole dish, then transfer the meat mixture to a bowl or blender and mash, shred or blitz the mixture until it has the consistency of a pâté. Scoop into six 8 cm (3¼ inch) ramekins or dariole moulds. Pour the rendered pork fat over the top to seal the rillettes. Refrigerate until the fat hardens, and eat with crusty bread, green salad, gherkins and walnuts.

500 g (1 lb 2 oz) pork neck

750 g (1 lb 10 oz) pork belly

350 g (12 oz) rabbit meat (leg, thigh and breast — ask your butcher)

1 tablespoon sea salt

2 bay leaves

1 rosemary sprig

16 juniper berries

5 cloves

20 black peppercorns

150 ml (5 fl oz) fruity beer, such as Hargreaves Hill Pale Ale

400 g (14 oz) pork fat, minced, (ground)

Chicken with garlic, olives and Saison Ale

SERVES 4

Cut the chicken into 10 pieces. The best way to do this is to cut the chicken in half lengthways, then cut the wings from the body. Remove the legs and thighs, separating the two and, last, cut the breast piece in half, keeping it on the bone.

Season the flour with the cumin, lemon pepper, cayenne pepper and some salt and pepper. Coat the chicken pieces in the seasoned flour and dust off the excess. Heat a large deep frying pan over medium heat. Add a splash of oil and cook the garlic cloves and shallots until slightly coloured, then remove from the pan. Add the anchovies and cook until melted, then add the chicken pieces and brown on all sides. Once the chicken is browned, pour in the beer and chicken stock and bring to a boil then add the olives, thyme and bay leaves and return the garlic and shallots to the pan. Reduce the heat to low and cook, covered, for about an hour.

When the chicken is cooked remove from the pan and keep warm. Return the pan to a high heat and reduce the sauce. Using the back of your wooden spoon, mash the whole cloves of garlic so that they mix into the sauce, thickening it. When the sauce has reduced to a consistency you are pleased with, serve the chicken and shallots accompanied by asparagus, broccoli, some roasted potatoes and the sauce.

1 chicken (about 1.6 kg–1.8 kg/
    3 lb 8 oz–4 lb)
plain (all-purpose) flour, for dusting
pinch of ground cumin
pinch of lemon pepper
pinch of cayenne pepper
olive oil
8 garlic cloves, peeled
8 French shallots, peeled
4–5 anchovy fillets
375 ml (13 fl oz/1½ cups) Beechworth
    Brewers Saison (a spicy farmhouse ale)
375 ml (13 fl oz/1½ cups) chicken stock
12 kalamata olives
6 thyme sprigs
4 bay leaves

Good bottleshops are now selling local and internationally made saisons. Keep an eye out for Saison Du Pont. It is a great beer.

Herb-crusted rack of lamb with asparagus purée

SERVES 2

400 g (14 oz) rack of lamb, about
  8 points
40 g (1½ oz/½ cup) sourdough
  breadcrumbs
80 g (2¾ oz/½ cup) macadamia nuts,
  finely chopped
1 garlic clove, crushed
grated zest of 1 lemon
1 teaspoon chopped rosemary
1 teaspoon chopped mint
1 tablespoon chopped chervil
1 tablespoon chopped oregano
3 teaspoons dijon mustard
olive oil
2 tomatoes, halved
10 asparagus spears, trimmed
6 garlic cloves, extra
125 ml (4 fl oz/½ cup) chicken stock

Preheat the oven to 180°C (350°F/Gas 4). Trim the lamb so that it is very lean with no fat or sinew, then season with salt and pepper.

To make the herb crust, put the breadcrumbs, macadamias, garlic, lemon zest and herbs in a bowl and mix well. With the rack lying ribs side down, spread the mustard on top of the lamb meat and then press a generous amount of the herb crumbs onto the mustard, packing it firmly.

Put a splash of olive oil in a roasting tin and carefully lay the rack on top of the oil, ribs down, crust up. Rub a splash of olive oil on to the tomatoes and four asparagus spears and spread them all out in the roasting tin. Put the extra garlic cloves into a foil pouch with a splash of olive oil. Twist the top of the foil to seal and put in the roasting tin. Roast for between 18 minutes (rare) and 28 minutes (well done) depending on your oven and your taste. Remove from the oven and rest the meat.

To make the asparagus purée, bring the stock to the boil in a small saucepan, then turn down to simmer. Cut the remaining six asparagus spears into five pieces each. Put the asparagus into the simmering chicken stock and cook until softened. Transfer the asparagus to a blender or food processor and blend until puréed using a little of the chicken stock to help break down the asparagus.

Put a large spoonful of the purée on each plate. To serve, cut the lamb into four sections, place two double chops on each plate along with the tomatoes, garlic cloves and asparagus.

Every now and then on my show, a chef like John Snelling from The Outpost Retreat, likes a dish I've cooked for them so much that they put it on their menu. This was one of those dishes. Gotta love that.

Roast standing rib eye

SERVES A FAMILY

1 untrimmed rib-eye scotch fillet end with
   two ribs on the back bone but no
   chine, about 2 kg–2.5 kg
   (4 lb 8 oz–5 lb 8 oz)
olive oil
2 tablespoons plain (all-purpose) flour
3 tablespoons red wine
3 tablespoons boiling water

MARINADE
2 tablespoons vegetable oil
2 garlic cloves, crushed
2 tablespoons dijon mustard
2 tablespoons red wine vinegar
2 tablespoons mixed fresh herbs,
   such as rosemary, marjoram
   and thyme

For the marinade: Using a mortar and pestle pound all the ingredients together until well combined and then rub all over the rib eye. Let it sit for a couple of hours.

Preheat the oven to 220°C (425°F/Gas 7). Add a splash of olive oil to a roasting tin and heat the tin over high heat. Brown the meat on all sides and then put in the oven for 20–25 minutes. Turn the oven down to 160°C (315°F/Gas 2–3) and cook for a further 15 minutes per 500 g (1 lb 2 oz) of meat for a medium–rare finish. When done remove from the oven and place in a warm dish, cover with foil and let the meat rest for 30 minutes before carving. Collect the juice for making gravy.

To make the gravy, spoon off the excess fat from the pan juices then put the roasting tin on the stove over a gentle heat. Add the flour to the pan but not directly into the juice — I tip my pan up a little so the juice stays down one end over the heat and I put the flour next to it but not in it. Use a fork to gradually work the flour a little at a time into the juice until it is all incorporated. The juice should now be like a thick paste. Add a generous slurp of red wine and an equal amount of boiling water from the kettle (if I am having peas with my roast I use the liquid that the peas were cooked in instead of boiling water). Again work this in with your fork until all of the liquid has been incorporated into a lovely velvety gravy. Taste for seasoning and add a little salt if necessary.

Serve the beef with roasted potatoes, pumpkin (winter squash), red onion, orange sweet potato and steamed green beans and, of course, the gravy.

A word of advice — make more than you think you will want because these ribs are very yummy. Since I was cooking these with Chris Helleren at her Les Chesselles Restaurant, I used ingredients from her pantry — well, actually her shop, as she sells lots of sauces and chutneys that she and other locals make — which you may not be able to get but you can use ingredients from your pantry. My usual ingredients for the marinade are: spring onion, sesame oil, hoisin sauce, barbecue sauce, mustard, hot mango chutney, sweet or hot chilli sauce and of, course, beer.

My wife and I usually have a Greek salad (see page 127) to accompany this finger-licking good dinner.

American-style barbecue ribs

SERVES 2 AS A MAIN

3 spring onions (scallions), roughly sliced
140 g (5 oz/½ cup) green tomato chutney
1 teaspoon wholegrain mustard
125 g (4½ oz/½ cup) hot chilli and garlic sauce
2 teaspoons sesame oil
125 ml (4 fl oz/½ cup) Coldstream Pilsner
2–3 racks of American-style pork ribs

Combine the spring onions, chutney, mustard, chilli and garlic sauce, sesame oil, pilsner and some salt and pepper in a large non-metallic bowl. Cut each rack of ribs into three equal-sized pieces and thoroughly coat all the pieces with the marinade. Leave to marinate for as long as possible, at least 2 hours but preferably overnight.

Preheat the oven to 180°C (350°F/Gas 4).

I call these American-style barbecue ribs because of the cut of ribs and the use of barbecue sauce. You can cook them on your barbecue or kettle barbecue as long as you have a lid. Cook with a direct heat and keep the temperature between 170–180°C (325°–350°F/Gas 3–4).

If you can't get Coldstream then use Coopers Original Pale Ale, Mountain Goat Pale, James Squire Pils or Matilda Bay Pilsener.

Rabbit fricassée with sweet potato mash

RECIPE BY CHRIS HELLEREN FROM LES CHESSELLES RESTAURANT, YARRA VALLEY

SERVES 4

Heat half the clarified butter in a large saucepan, season the rabbit and brown in batches, turning once. Remove from the saucepan and set aside. Add the remaining butter to the saucepan and brown the mushrooms.

Put the rabbit back into the saucepan with the mushrooms. Add the verjuice and boil for a couple of minutes before adding the stock and bouquet garni. Cover the saucepan tightly and simmer gently over very low heat for 40 minutes.

For the mash: Put the sweet potato, onion and Vegeta in a saucepan of water, bring to the boil and cook until the sweet potato is tender. Drain well, then return to the pan. Add the butter and mash well.

Meanwhile, heat the oil in a small saucepan. Remove the leaves from the bunch of sage and drop them, a few at a time, into the hot oil. The leaves will immediately start to bubble around the edges. Cook them for 30 seconds, or until bright green and crispy. Make sure you don't overheat the oil or cook the leaves for too long or they will turn black and taste burnt. Drain the leaves on paper towels and sprinkle with salt.

Lift the cooked rabbit and mushrooms out of the saucepan and keep warm. Discard the bouquet garni. Remove the pan from the heat, mix together the cream and egg yolks and stir quickly into the stock. Return to very low heat and cook, stirring, for about 5 minutes to thicken slightly (don't let the sauce boil or the eggs will scramble). Season with salt and pepper.

To serve, scoop the mash into a bowl, then top with the rabbit pieces and mushrooms. Pour the sauce over the top, then garnish with crispy sage leaves.

60 g (2¼ oz) clarified butter
1.5 kg (3 lb 5 oz) rabbit, cut into 8 pieces
200 g (7 oz) button mushrooms, sliced
4 tablespoons verjuice
170 ml (5½ fl oz/⅔ cup) chicken stock
1 bouquet garni
4 tablespoons olive oil
1 small bunch of sage
125 ml (4½ fl oz/½ cup) thick cream
2 egg yolks

MASH
2 large sweet potatoes, diced
1 onion, chopped
1 tablespoon Vegeta or other
    powdered seasoning
20 g (¾ oz) butter

Bouillabaisse

Heat a splash of olive oil in a large, deep frying pan over medium heat. Add the leek, fennel and garlic and cook until translucent (8–10 minutes), then add the carrot and potato and fry for about 5 minutes or so, giving it a mix every now and then. Add the tomato, saffron, orange zest, bay leaves, parsley stalks and the Pernod and cook for another 5 or so minutes to allow the flavours to combine. Pour in the stock and gently simmer for 20–30 minutes or until the potato and carrot are cooked.

Add the firmest fish first, which will take the longest to cook. So add the boarfish first and then let the soup come back up to the boil and the fish to change colour before adding the trumpeter and following the same procedure before adding the snapper. Add the snapper, flounder and mussels and simmer until all the fish is cooked and the mussels open. To finish, throw in a generous pinch of chopped dill and parsley. Discard any mussels that remain tightly closed. Remove the parsley stalks.

Cut slices of the sourdough and drizzle both sides of the bread with olive oil and then grill them over the barbecue or grill plate on the stove. Turn when coloured and rub the cooked surface with the cut side of the raw clove of garlic. When the other side is cooked rub it with the garlic.

Serve the soup in large bowls, making sure each bowl gets some of each fillet of fish and mussels. Garnish with the extra parsley and place a piece of the garlicky toast on the side.

olive oil

1 leek, white part only, thinly sliced

1 baby fennel bulb, thinly sliced

2 garlic cloves, thinly sliced

1 carrot, cut into small dice

1 potato, cut into small dice

400 g (14 oz) tin chopped tomatoes

15 saffron threads, softened in a little
    fish stock

1 piece orange zest

3 bay leaves

1 bunch parsley stalks

3 tablespoons Pernod

3 litres (105 fl oz/12 cups) fish stock
    preferably home-made but a good-
    quality store-bought one is fine

500 g (1 lb 2 oz) fresh fish fillets, cut into
    2 cm (¾ inch) cubes — approximately
    1 each of boarfish, trumpeter
    and snapper (or use any firm white-
    fleshed fish)

1 whole flounder, gutted and chopped
    into three pieces

10 black mussels, cleaned and
    hairy beards removed

2 tablespoons finely chopped dill

2 tablespoons finely chopped parsley

1 loaf sourdough

olive oil, for drizzling

1 garlic clove, peeled and cut in half

chopped, parsley, extra, to serve

Steak tartare

SERVES 6 AS A STARTER

2–3 anchovy fillets, chopped

1 teaspoon dijon mustard

1 tablespoon olive oil, plus extra, for drizzling

2 tablespoons high–alcohol beer

1 egg yolk

2 tablespoons tomato, garlic and chilli chutney

½ small red onion, very thinly sliced

1 tablespoon salted capers, drained, rinsed, and chopped

1 tablespoon chopped cornichons

2 tablespoons chopped flat-leaf (Italian) parsley

½ teaspoon salt

350 g (12 oz) steak sirloin

½ apple, finely chopped

1 tablespoon finely chopped flat-leaf (Italian) parsley

2 tablespoons finely chopped roasted hazelnuts

Mix the anchovies, mustard, oil, beer, egg yolk and chutney in a bowl until well combined, then add the onion, capers, cornichons and parsley, mix again and season with the salt.

The meat should be chopped finely using a sharp knife — if you can't get it as fine as you want then once you have cut it up quite fine, blitz it in a food processor for a second or two at a time and do this a maximum of three times. You do not want to do it for long or it will heat the meat. Add the meat to the bowl with the anchovy mixture and fold them through so that they are evenly and well mixed. Taste and adjust the seasoning if needed — it can be on the salty side.

Serve on a plate, scatter with the apple, parsley and hazelnuts and drizzle a little olive oil around the plate. Accompany with some lightly toasted bread.

You need to use really top-quality beef to make steak tartare. You could put it through a mincer (grinder) but I like the texture that finely chopping the meat gives.

Drunken quinces

RECIPE BY WINNIE JONES FROM MOUNT BELLEVUE WELSH CATTLE STUD, MYRRHEE

SERVES 8

Peel, quarter and core the quinces. Place the fruit in a saucepan and sprinkle it with the sugar, cloves and vanilla. Pour in the red wine, cover with a lid, bring to the boil and turn down to a simmer. After 30 minutes, test the fruit — if it is just firm to the touch, remove the quinces from the pan, reserving the juice. If the fruit is not ready, keep testing every 5 minutes or so — this could take up to 1 hour for large fruit.

Turn up the heat, and reduce the pan juices for 15–20 minutes until they thicken to a delicious purple syrup. Add more sugar if required. Pour the liquid over the quinces.

Place 3 quince quarters in each serving dish with a good dollop of cream and garnish with a sprig of mint.

6 quinces
345 g (12 oz/1½ cups) caster (superfine) sugar, to taste
8 cloves
2 vanilla beans, split and scraped or 2 teaspoons natural vanilla extract
750 ml (26 fl oz) bottle red wine
thick cream, to serve
mint sprigs, to garnish

My daughter Elise's double-dipped chocolate strawberries

SERVES 4

Wash and dry the strawberries, keeping the leafy part intact — you'll need this to act as a handle later. Line a plate with baking paper.

Grab a saucepan and fill it with water about one-third of the way up the side and put it on a low heat. Get a heatproof bowl that can rest easily on the top without touching the water and place it over the saucepan. Add the dark chocolate and melt, stirring occasionally.

When the chocolate is melted, take the strawberries (holding them by the leaves) and dip one at a time into the chocolate. If it gets a bit fiddly or the leaves pull away, use a toothpick or skewer inserted into the strawberry to help dip more efficiently. Place the dipped strawberries onto the plate that is covered with baking paper so the strawberries are easy to peel off when set.

Leave the strawberries to set in the fridge or in a cool place before repeating the process with the white chocolate. For an added touch, press a mint leaf on the flat side of the dipped strawberry before being left to set. Return the strawberries to the fridge to allow the chocolate to harden.

500 g (1 lb 2 oz) large strawberries
250 g (9 oz) dark or milk chocolate, chopped
125 g (4½ oz) white chocolate, chopped
1 handful of mint leaves

One of life's great pleasures is cooking with my children. I have three daughters and I have taught them how to cook. My eldest daughter, Elise, helped me create and test some of my recipes as well as make these strawberries for the show.

TASMANIA

A lasting memory I have from Tassie is cooking at Binalong Bay with chef Tom Dicker. We cooked on the beach over a fire we built. It was a white fish with chilli sambal and it was glorious. Yes, it is about the food but sometimes the location can just make the experience all the more magical.

Mercurio's Menu shot two episodes in Tasmania for series one which featured one episode in the north around Launceston and the other down south around Hobart. Sadly, we didn't make it down to Tassie for series two. However, as I write this I have just finished shooting two more episodes in Tasmania for series three. Those recipes won't be in this book but they are great and well worth waiting for when series three hits the airwaves. Several years ago I did another food show where we shot four one-hour episodes in Tasmania, so all up I have shot eight shows in the state and I happily confess that Tasmania with its producers, chefs, food, wine and beer scene is my all-time favourite place to go.

I started coming to Tasmania back in the early 1980s while on tour with the Sydney Dance Company. My first food memory from then is of the scallop pies I would buy from a little pie shop in Hobart just down from the wharf, they were delicious and had big, juicy, plump scallops in them — you can still buy them today. I also love going down to Victoria Dock and Constitution Dock and buying fish and chips from the little floating fish and chip shops there and sitting with my legs dangling over the water, throwing the occasional chip to the seagulls. It is there that the Mures fishing boats pull in to unload their catch of fish for the restaurant that sits proudly and prominently in the middle of the wharf. I was lucky enough to go out on the boat for about 37 nautical kilometres and help catch some fish — about one tonne on that day, and even luckier to take one to the restaurant and cook it.

I found the largest and the best cherries I have ever had on Bruny Island which is about 40 kilometres out of Hobart. One of the great things about Tasmania is nothing is more than a few hours' drive away, whether it's Joe Bennett's oysters which are beautiful, plump and harvested every morning, or Grandvewe Cheeses, where you can buy cheese, yoghurt and gelato all made from sheep's milk, or Michael Carne's award-winning fudge.

It's the same up north around Launceston. There, I met a chef, Daniel Alps, who had worked the driving thing to his advantage. You see, he had all the producers drive to him bringing in all their goodies for him to look at and see what he would put on the menu for the day. The best thing about it was that the food was picked that morning and by lunchtime, it was on someone's plate in the dining room. I really enjoyed cooking with Daniel as his approach was all about being inspired by what was local and what was fresh. On the day I was there, a local venison farmer brought in some beautiful venison loin — so you can guess what we cooked up.

Provençal-style vegetables

RECIPE BY DANIEL ALPS FROM STRATHLYNN, ROSEVEARS

SERVES 6

In a saucepan over medium heat place the butter, cherry tomatoes, tarragon and some sea salt and white pepper. Cook until the tomatoes soften and reduce. Set aside until needed.

Add the olive oil to a frying pan and sauté the zucchini and eggplant in batches over medium–high heat until golden. Drain on paper towel.

Sweat the onion and garlic in a saucepan over medium heat in a little oil until translucent. Add the tomatoes with all the buttery juice and the herbs, capers, eggplant, zucchini, marinated capsicums, and some more sea salt and white pepper. Continue to cook gently so that all of the flavours combine.

In a saucepan of boiling water blanch the snow peas and beans for a few minutes, and then add to the vegetable mix. Add the olives and basil and serve.

60 g (2¼ oz) butter
250 g (9 oz) cherry tomatoes
½ bunch of tarragon, leaves only
olive oil
3 zucchini (courgettes), halved lengthways and sliced into half moons
2 eggplants (aubergines), halved lengthways and sliced
1 brown onion, sliced
1 garlic clove, crushed
1 teaspoon salted capers, drained and rinsed
100 g (3½ oz) marinated red capsicums (peppers), drained
100 g (3½ oz) snow peas (mangetout)
100 g (3½ oz) yellow beans
100 g (3½ oz) green beans
1 tablespoon sliced kalamata olives
1 bunch of basil, leaves torn

Simple, fresh and locally grown vegetables — picked and delivered that morning, cooked and served that afternoon. It doesn't get much better than that!

This recipe began as an experiment to see how different beers affect, change and enhance beer-battered fish. You can either conduct the experiment for yourself or just choose one beer for the batter. If you do want to try a few different beers, I suggest using four, including a wheat beer, a pale ale, a stout or dark beer and a pilsner.

If you just want to have some beer-battered fish for dinner then get a couple of fillets of fish (flake, blue-eye trevalla, wild barramundi, goldband snapper or even some flathead tails) and keep them whole.

Beer-battered fish   SERVES 2

2 x 250 g–300 g (9 oz–10½ oz) firm fish
    fillets, skin and bones removed, cut
    into smaller pieces if desired
lemon wedges, to serve

BATTER
60 g (2¼ oz/½ cup) plain
    (all-purpose) flour
200 ml (7 fl oz) bottle of beer
oil, for deep-frying

For the batter: Put the flour in a bowl, add a good pinch of sea salt and then pour in some or all of the beer and whisk. The amount of beer you pour in depends on the thickness you want your batter to be — a thick batter in the bowl means a thick batter on your fish.

Once your batter is done, drop your pieces of fish into it, coating them well. Fill a deep-fryer, wok or heavy-based saucepan one-third full of oil and heat to 180°C (350°F), or until a cube of bread dropped into the oil browns in 15 seconds. If you are using more than one beer, cook each batch of fish separately in the oil as the idea is to taste and compare each batter and if you cook them together you will have a little bit of trouble differentiating which is which. Remove from the oil and drain on some crumpled paper towel. Serve with lemon wedges

As you eat, take note of how the different characters in the different beers enhances the fish. Or just enjoy with a beer of your choice. Cheers.

If you take the beer-batter challenge divide your fish portion into four — and make smaller batters using four different beers.

Mures Upper Deck blue-eye recipe

RECIPE BY MATT DEAKIN FROM MURES UPPER DECK, HOBART

SERVES 6

Preheat the oven to 200°C (400°F/Gas 6). To make the balsamic juice, reduce the veal stock with thyme to 300 ml (10½ fl oz), then strain. In another saucepan, sweat the shallots and garlic in a drizzle of olive oil for 5 minutes over medium heat. Add the port and balsamic vinegar and reduce to 200 ml (7 fl oz), then strain and add to the reduced veal stock. Season with salt and pepper and leave over very low heat while you cook the vegetables and fish.

Put the potatoes in a roasting tin, drizzle with olive oil and season with salt and pepper. Roast for 25–30 minutes. About 6–7 minutes before the potatoes are done, add the zucchini flowers, beans and tomatoes, a little more seasoning and another drizzle of olive oil.

At the same time place your blue-eye on a baking tray with a little splash of olive oil and salt and pepper and grill (broil) or bake for 5–6 minutes or until just cooked through.

To serve, place the roasted vegetables on six plates, place a fillet of blue-eye on top of each and drizzle over the balsamic jus. Serve with some lemon wedges.

12 potatoes, halved
olive oil
12 small zucchini (courgette) flowers
300 g (10½ oz) green beans
30 cherry tomatoes
6 x 180 g (6¼ oz) blue-eye trevalla fillets
lemon wedges, to serve

BALSAMIC JUS
600 ml (21 fl oz) veal stock
5 thyme sprigs
6 French shallots, sliced
2 garlic cloves, sliced
olive oil
500 ml (17 fl oz/2 cups) port
100 ml (3½ fl oz) balsamic vinegar

Roasted venison with baby beetroot and Persian feta salad

RECIPE BY DANIEL ALPS FROM STRATHLYNN, ROSEVEARS

SERVES 2

2 pieces venison loin,
    approximately 250 g–300 g
    (9 oz–10½ oz) each
olive oil

SALAD
300 g (10½ oz) baby beetroot (beets)
150 g (5½ oz) speck
1 small bunch of flat-leaf (Italian) parsley,
    coarsely chopped
6 cubes of Persian feta cheese
1 small handful of baby beetroot
    (beet) shoots
3 tablespoons extra virgin olive oil
2 tablespoons balsamic vinegar

For the salad: Put the baby beetroot in a large saucepan of salted water, bring to the boil and cook for 20 minutes or until tender. Drain, when cool enough to handle, peel and halve. Meanwhile, cut the fat off the piece of speck and place the fat in a hot frying pan. Dice the rest of the speck and add to the pan. Fry until just crispy.

In a bowl, combine the baby beetroot, fried speck, parsley and some salt and pepper and toss together. Tip the beetroot onto a plate and crumble the feta over the top. Garnish with the beetroot shoots.

Combine the olive oil and balsamic in a bowl, whisk well and then pour over the beetroot salad.

For the venison: Preheat the oven to 200°C (400°F/Gas 6). Season the venison with sea salt and white pepper. Heat a splash of oil in a frying pan over high heat, add the pieces of venison and seal both sides until golden brown. Remove from the pan and place into the oven for 6 minutes, turning after 3 minutes. Remove from the oven and rest for at least 6 minutes or until ready to serve.

Slice the roasted venison across the grain and place on top of some beetroot salad. Spoon the dressing over the beetroot salad and venison.

When I cooked at the Strathlynn in Rosevears with head chef Daniel Alps, we knew we'd cook venison but not what we'd put with it. We stood in the coolroom and looked at the great produce in there and together came up with this recipe — easy!

Crayfish and raspberry terrine

SERVES 10 AS A STARTER

100 g (3½ oz/2¼ cups) baby English
   spinach leaves
½ onion, finely chopped
olive oil
250 g (9 oz/2 cups) raspberries
1 teaspoon icing (confectioners') sugar
100 g (3½ oz) crustless white bread,
   torn into small pieces
125 ml (4 fl oz/½ cup) cream, for whipping
4 egg whites
300 g (10½ oz) white fish
   (such as ling or flathead)
300 g (10½ oz) pink fish (such as ocean
   trout or Atlantic salmon)
1 tablespoon chopped dill
250 ml (9 fl oz/1 cup) cream, extra
1 long red chilli, chopped
splash of Tabasco sauce
1 crayfish or lobster tail, about
   250 g–350 g (9 oz–12 oz)

Preheat the oven to 150°C (300°F/Gas 2). Lightly oil a 22 cm (8½ inch) long x 8 cm (3¼ inch) wide x 7 cm (2¾ inch) deep terrine tin and line with a double layer of plastic wrap so there is some hanging over the edge. You will make two separate fish mousses, one with the white fish and one with the pink.

Blanch the spinach in boiling water for about 30 seconds, then remove to a bowl of iced water and allow it to chill. Drain the spinach, place it in a food processor and blend to a smooth paste. Remove from the blender and put in a sieve over a bowl so that the liquid will drain away.

Fry the onion in a splash of olive oil until fragrant and translucent but not browned.

Reduce the raspberries in a saucepan over gentle heat with the icing sugar until they have broken down — give them a bit of a squash with a spoon to assist. Set aside to cool.

Take two bowls and place half of the bread pieces into each bowl, then pour half the cream into each bowl. Beat half of the egg whites for about 10 seconds and put in one bowl. Repeat with the other egg whites and add them to the second bowl. Give the ingredients in each bowl a good mix and then let sit while you prepare the fish. Finely chop the fish, keeping the white and pink fish separate.

To make the white fish mousse, put the fish into a food processor and blend until well minced. Add one of the bowls of the bread, cream and egg-white mix and blend until well combined. Add half of the onion, all of the well-drained spinach and the dill, some salt and pepper and then blend until well combined. If the fish mix forms into a ball in the blender do not blend any longer. Turn out the mixture into a large bowl. Beat the extra cream to soft peaks and fold half of the whipped cream through the white fish mixture. This mixture will now be a nice green colour.

To make the pink fish mousse, follow the same procedure as the white but use the chilli and the Tabasco instead of the spinach and dill. You will now have a nice orange/pink fish mousse with a slight bite to it, add a little salt and pepper. Fold through the remaining whipped cream.

To assemble: Put the pink mousse in the prepared terrine tin first, filling the terrine tin up to no more than halfway. Bang the terrine tin firmly on the bench to settle the mixture. Next take your fresh uncooked crayfish tail, cut it in in half lengthways, and roll it around in 2 tablespoons of the raspberry mixture so that it is well coated, then carefully place the two pieces down the middle of the terrine tin on top of the mousse. Reserve the rest of the raspberry mixture for serving. Gently push the tail pieces into the mixture so that it sinks halfway. Next carefully place some of the second (green) fish mixture against the side of the terrine tin to fill in the gap between the crayfish and the side of the terrine tin — this makes sure there is a definite line between the green and the pink. Then cover the rest of the crayfish and fill to the top of the terrine tin with the green mousse. Bang the tin again several times firmly on a bench to settle. Fold over the plastic wrap to enclose.

Place the terrine tin on top of a folded tea towel (dish towel) in a roasting tin and then fill with boiling water until it is halfway up the sides of the tin. Bake for about 40 minutes or until the internal temperature of the terrine reaches 65°C (150°F). Once cooked, remove from the roasting tin and let cool, then refrigerate overnight.

Turn out of the terrine tin and slice about 1 cm (½ inch) thick. Dip a pastry brush into the raspberries and paint a thick stroke across a plate. Place the terrine slice halfway over the raspberries. Serve with a slice of toasted sourdough rubbed with a raw garlic clove and some mixed greens lightly dressed with oil and balsamic vinegar.

More than a few people, including the camera crew and chefs, looked at me as if I'd gone a little crazy when I designed this dish. The proof was in the pudding or in this case, the terrine. When we finished shooting everyone devoured my creation!

Whitefish with chilli sambal

RECIPE BY TOM DICKER AT ANGASI RESTAURANT, BINALONG BAY

SERVES 2

4 eggs
4–6 white fish fillets, depending on their
    size (for instance, you could use
    6 flathead tails at about 80 g/2¾
    each or 4 ling or whiting fillets at
    about 150 g/5½ oz each)
olive oil
375 g (13 oz/2 cups) cooked basmati rice
kecap manis, to serve
coriander (cilantro) leaves, chopped,
    to garnish

CHILLI SAMBAL
2 large red chillies, roughly chopped
1 large tomato, halved and then sliced
1 teaspoon shrimp paste
2 garlic cloves, chopped
2 tablespoons grated palm sugar (jaggery)

For the chilli sambal: Use a mortar and pestle to pound the chillies, then add the tomato and pound, breaking it down. Next add the shrimp paste, garlic and palm sugar and pound away until you have a paste.

Boil the eggs in a saucepan to your liking — 4 minutes if you want them slightly runny or 6 minutes if you want them hard. Run under cold water, peel, then chop and set aside.

Season the fish fillets with salt and pepper. Add a splash of olive oil to a frying pan over high heat and cook the fish for 2–3 minutes on each side.

Pile the rice, chopped eggs and the fish onto your plate and dress with the chilli sambal, drizzle over some kecap manis and garnish with the coriander leaves.

Cherry cheesecake with sheep's milk ricotta

SERVES 8–12

For the base: Preheat the oven to 180°C (350°F/Gas 4). Process the biscuits in a blender until all broken up into fine crumbs, then transfer to a bowl. Add the mixed spice to the melted butter and mix well, then add the butter to the biscuit crumbs and mix thoroughly, making sure there are no dry spots.

Line the base of a 22 cm (8½ inch) spring-form cake tin with foil and then assemble the tin and grease the bottom and side. Press the biscuit crumbs on to the bottom and halfway up the side of the cake tin. Put in the fridge while you make the filling.

For the filling: Beat the cheeses together with electric beaters, then beat in the sugar and cornflour. Add one egg at a time and beat thoroughly before adding the next. Lastly, beat in the sour cream.

Place a little of the mixture in the tin and spread it out to cover the bottom of the cake tin, then add enough morello cherries to cover the base (about 200 g/7 oz). Pour the rest of the filling on top of the cherries. Bake for about 1¼ hours. Check to see if it is cooked by piercing with a wooden skewer — if the skewer comes out clean the cake is done; if it comes out wet with some mixture on it cook a little longer, then check again. Remove from the oven and let cool completely.

For the sauce: Pour the reserved cherry juice into a saucepan and add the sugar and 2 tablespoons of the port. Bring to the boil, stirring, until the sugar has dissolved, then reduce the heat and simmer until the sauce has reduced by at least half and is nice and syrupy. Taste the sauce and add the rest of the port and a little more sugar if you think it needs it. Set aside to cool completely.

Scatter the fresh or thawed cherries over the top of the cheesecake. Cut a slice, put on a plate and drizzle a little of the sauce around the plate — you won't need too much. Serve with a dollop of cream on the side.

BASE

310 g (11 oz) butternut snap biscuits (oat and coconut cookies), about 1¼ packets

1¼ teaspoons mixed (pumpkin pie) spice

100 g (3½ oz) butter, melted, plus extra, for greasing

FILLING

250 g (9 oz/1 cup) cream cheese, softened

250 g (9 oz/1 cup) sheep's milk ricotta or cow's milk ricotta (see note)

175 g (6 oz) caster (superfine) sugar

2 tablespoons cornflour (cornstarch)

3 eggs

250 g (9 oz/1 cup) sour cream

700 g (1 lb 9 oz) jar pitted morello cherries, drained and juice reserved

SAUCE

250 ml (9 fl oz/1 cup) reserved juice from the morello cherries

1 tablespoon raw (demerara) sugar

2–6 tablespoons port, to taste

320 g (11¼ oz) fresh or defrosted cherries, pitted, to serve

The sheep's milk ricotta adds a grainy texture to the cheesecake which works really well.

NEW ZEALAND

There is a strong focus in New Zealand on super fresh, high-quality and local ingredients – and now consumers like me expect to find that wherever we go to eat – and this vibrant country is delivering.

I only shot two episodes in New Zealand: one on the North Island in and around Wellington and the other on the South Island featuring the Otago region. I have been lucky enough to have been travelling to and from New Zealand since the early 1980s when I was a young dancer touring the world. Back then, going out to dinner was not something you lingered over — possibly that had something to do with the fact that on a dancer's wage you certainly couldn't afford to eat at the high-class establishments but also because food back then wasn't all that good. This was true of touring country regions in Australia also — you could forget getting a decent meal in Orange in the early '80s, now days, it's no problem. Over the years, and the trips, I have noticed the food scene in both Australia and New Zealand grow and then blossom into a multicultural and exciting industry that without a doubt is on par with anywhere in the world. A lot of New Zealand chefs (and Australian for that matter) went overseas and worked in some of the best restaurants in Europe and then returned home bringing with them their experiences, expectations and desires to create the best restaurants and produce they could.

In Wellington I took a walking tour with Cath Cordwell who runs Zest Food Tours. We walked around for a couple of hours and in that time I tasted world-class chocolates, some of the best fresh-roasted coffee around and popped into a family run grocery store where you could buy a diverse range of produce from jams, chutneys and sauces to rabbit, venison, crabs, paua, sea urchin and an array of cheeses and breads — it was mind-boggling. I also hooked up with a great chef, Al Brown, who took me for a drive in his old Holden out to a beach where we met a couple of fishermen who gave us some of their catch on the proviso we cooked them lunch. Al and I built a fire on the beach using driftwood and then proceeded to cook up a great lunch of fish that had been caught only hours before — it was fantastic, and for me, a very special memory that I will have from my visit to the North Island.

I had fun in my first stop, Otago, Queenstown as it's the adventure capital of the world. It's a beautiful area and has a vibrant food scene. I attended a cooking school where I cooked up some pheasant for Debbie who told me off for being messy and gave me four out of ten for my plating skills but still managed to polish off my dish. And I met the most remarkable, well-known and loved local, Fleur, who took me down to the seaside by her restaurant. We picked mussels off the rocks, chatted about life and then took the mussels back to her place to cook them. Her chef also cooked me some mutton bird, which is actually a delicacy in New Zealand, but is certainly not to me and that's why it's not in the book!

This dish is to be enjoyed 'bathing' in plenty of the best-quality oil you can get your hands on. Don't settle for anything less.

Saffron, bay leaf and fennel potatoes

RECIPE BY DEBBIE CROMPTON FROM PUNATAPU LODGE, OTAGO

SERVES 4 AS A SIDE

Preheat the oven to 180°C (350°F/Gas 4). In a heavy-based flameproof casserole dish or ovenproof frying pan, begin by gently cooking the chopped onion, garlic and sliced fennel in the extra virgin olive oil.

Add the bay leaves, and break up the saffron in the palm of your hand before adding to the dish. Do not allow to brown, but rather 'sweat' the vegetables slowly — the slower this is done the better the flavour will be.

Slice the potatoes into 5 mm (¼ inch) slices (skin on is fine) and add to the dish. Mix well, and add plenty of freshly ground black pepper and salt. Mix again to ensure the salt and pepper are evenly distributed throughout the dish. If you like, add another slug of olive oil — the potatoes shouldn't be too dry.

Cover the dish with a lid and put into the oven for 40 minutes until the potatoes are just tender when tested with a fork. It pays to mix again once during cooking to make sure the flavours of the bay leaves, and fennel have infused evenly, and the saffron has stained everything a glorious rusty orange.

1 onion, chopped,
4 garlic cloves, crushed
1 large fennel bulb, thinly sliced
250 ml (9 fl oz/1 cup) extra virgin olive oil
8 fresh bay leaves
2 pinches Ida Valley saffron threads or other saffron
800 g–1 kg (1 lb 12 oz–2 lb 4 oz) small waxy potatoes, such as kipfler (fingerling)

This is a classic example of utilising great local ingredients to their best advantage. If you make this using the very best produce it will be absolutely delicious.

This recipe is not an exact science in terms of the amounts of each ingredient — if you love olives put more than eight per piece of fish, if you are not keen on capers use a teaspoon between the two pieces of fish instead of one each.

Hapuku (groper) in foil cooked on coals

SERVES 2

50 g (1¾ oz) butter
1 lemon, sliced
1 bunch of dill
2 hapuku (groper) or other firm
   white fish fillets, about 300 g
   (10½ oz) in total
4 French shallots, thinly sliced
250 g (9 oz) cherry tomatoes, diced
2 teaspoons salted capers, drained
   and rinsed
16 kalamata olives, squeeze out the pips
   and tear the olives with your hands
8–10 basil leaves, torn
cirtus olive oil or plain olive oil

As the foil packages of fish are going to lie directly on hot coals you will want to double the foil so as not to get any tears. Take four pieces of foil large enough to wrap the fish in and lay two of the pieces on the bench, then top with the other pieces so you have two lots of foil. Smear or rub the butter onto the foil then lay out 3 lemon slices and top with about half of the dill. Now lay the groper fillet on top of the dill. Scatter with half the shallots, tomato, capers, olives and basil. Drizzle some citrus olive oil over everything and season with a few twists of freshly ground black pepper. Wrap the foil, bringing each side up and twisting together to create a neat, tightly sealed parcel. Repeat with the remaining ingredients in the second foil package. The fish will steam as well as roast in these packages.

Place the packages on hot coals and cook for about 10 minutes. Carefully open the foil and check if the fish is ready by flaking with a fork — if the flesh flakes, it is ready. If the fish is not cooked, re-wrap it and cook for a little longer. Eat directly out of the foil package savouring all of the lovely juice created by the fish, butter, lemon and tomato.

We built a fire on the beach and prepared all the food on the boot of an old Holden car. We cooked on the open fire and ate watching the waves roll in. It was a magnificent day!

Salad of dory ceviche, blood sausage and grapefruit

SERVES 2

For the cabernet syrup: Place the vinegar and sugar in a small saucepan over low heat and stir to dissolve the sugar. Increase the heat and reduce for 10 minutes, or until syrupy. Set aside to cool.

Place the sliced dory into a bowl, then add the lime juice, mix and let it sit for about 5 minutes, then drain off the excess juice.

In a hot frying pan with some olive oil, fry the chorizo and blood sausage until coloured and crispy.

In a salad bowl combine the fennel, rocket, grapefruit segments and coriander and give it all a good mix then add in the chorizo, blood sausage and ceviche of dory and mix through again. Dress with a drizzle of citrus oil and a drizzle of cabernet syrup, mix and then serve.

200 g (7 oz) fillet of john dory, thinly sliced
juice of 1 lime
80 g (2¾ oz) fresh chorizo sausage,
    finely diced
80 g (2¾ oz) blood sausage (also called
    black pudding), finely diced
1 baby fennel, very thinly sliced including
    the tips
1 handful of baby rocket (arugula)
1 ruby grapefruit, segmented
1 handful of coriander (cilantro)
    leaves, chopped
citrus olive oil or plain olive oil

CABERNET SYRUP
125 ml (4 fl oz/½ cup) cabernet
    sauvignon vinegar
110 g (3¾ oz/½ cup) sugar

Lamb with artichokes and capers

SERVES 2

250 g–300 g (9 oz–10½ oz) lamb
   backstrap or loin fillet

olive oil

3 spring onions (scallions)

50 g (1¾ oz) prosciutto, slices cut into
   thin strips

1 tablespoon salted capers, drained
   and rinsed

3 tablespoons dry white wine

3 tablespoons chicken stock

340 g (11¾ oz) jar marinated
   artichoke hearts, drained
   and halved

1 handful of flat-leaf (Italian) parsley,
   leaves picked and half the
   parsley chopped

Cut the lamb into pieces about 3 cm (1¼ inches) long and 2 cm (¾ inch) wide. Heat a splash of olive oil in a frying pan over high heat and add the lamb. Season with salt and black pepper and cook until nicely coloured but not completely cooked, then remove from the pan and keep warm. As you are going to return the lamb to the pan with the other ingredients it is important not to cook the lamb all the way through at this stage or it will overcook and become tough when it is added to the sauce.

Add a little more oil to the pan if needed and, when hot, add the spring onions and prosciutto and fry until the spring onions are softened. Add the capers and heat through, then splash in the wine and stock. Bring to the boil, add the artichokes and simmer to reduce the sauce by half. Return the lamb (and any juices from the lamb) to the pan and let it warm through with the sauce for a few minutes, giving it all a good mix to combine the flavours. To finish, scatter over the chopped parsley and mix it in well so that it combines through the sauce and then serve in a bowl garnished with the remaining parsley.

This is a super simple, very tasty, rustic, Italian-style dish you will love.

Seafood and wheat beer chowder

SERVES 2

10 black mussels, on the shell
10 cockles, on the shell
10 scallops, on the shell
10 whelks (sea snails), in the shell
olive oil
1 leek, white part only, chopped
2 celery stalks, diced
2 garlic cloves, finely diced
1 red chilli, finely diced
500 ml (17 fl oz/2 cups) bottle of Three
    Boys Wheat beer (see note)
250 ml (9 fl oz/1 cup) chicken stock
2 tomatoes, peeled, seeded and diced
1 fresh corn cob, corn kernels cut off
    the cob
3 tablespoons cream
2 tablespoons finely chopped coriander
    (cilantro) leaves
1 large banded morwong or red moki
    fillet, about 300 g (10½ oz)
1 tablespoon finely snipped chives
sourdough, to serve

Scrub the mussels and pull out the hairy beards and discard any broken mussels, or open ones that don't close when tapped on the work surface. Rinse all the shellfish well.

In a frying pan large enough to hold all of the ingredients add a splash of olive oil and gently fry the leek until softened. Add the celery and fry until softened and then add the garlic and chilli and fry for several minutes. Pour in the beer, bring to a boil. Add the cockles, cover the pan with a lid and bring the liquid back to the boil. Next add the mussels, again cover the pan and cook for 4–5 minutes, or until the mussels have opened, then add the scallops and whelks, cover with a lid and cook for a couple of minutes. Add the chicken stock, tomato, corn and some salt and pepper. Give it all a good stir and check for seasoning. Bring the liquid back to the boil and add the cream and coriander. Give it all a mix and again and check seasoning and adjust if necessary. Discard any mussels or cockles that remain closed.

While the chowder is coming back to the boil, season the banded morwong fillet on both sides with salt and pepper. Add a splash of olive oil to a frying pan over high heat or hot barbecue plate and cook the fish for 3 minutes on each side.

To serve, place the cooked fish fillet in a large shallow serving bowl, then pour the chowder over it. Garnish with the chopped chives. Serve in the middle of the table and everyone can help themselves. Soak up the chowder with some fresh crusty sourdough.

In Australia, use Feral White, Hoegaarden Ale, Redback Original or Holgate White Ale in place of the Three Boys, which can only be found in NZ.

Aussies are more likely to know paua as abalone and buttie as sandwich. When Al made these sandwiches for me on the beach over an open fire they were absolutely delicious, even more so because Al had dived for the paua only an hour earlier. On that day he also added some mayonnaise to the bread as well as the butter which I loved — you can do that as an option if you like. Just use a good store-bought mayonnaise.

Paua buttie

RECIPE BY AL BROWN, WELLINGTON

MAKES 8

To prepare the paua, ask your fishmonger to remove the paua from the shell and give it a clean. Then at home take a sharp knife and slice the paua into as thin slivers as possible.

First, butter your bread — you'll need 16 slices for 8 butties.

It's best to sauté the paua in two batches. Heat up a frying pan, sauté pan or barbecue hotplate. Once hot, add a little oil and then your onion and garlic and sauté until golden. Remove from the pan into a bowl. Wipe the pan clean and place it back on the heat. Add a touch of olive oil, then half the batch of paua. Season with salt and pepper. Cook the paua for no longer than a couple of minutes, turning after it starts to caramelise. Remove from the pan and cook the second batch. Once cooked, return all the paua and the onion mixture to the pan. Sprinkle the chilli and coriander over the paua, mix through, add a couple of tablespoons of butter and a squeeze of lemon juice to finish. Cook for another 30 seconds, then remove the paua from the pan. Now lay out 8 pieces of bread and divide the paua onto each piece. Finally add half a handful of rocket to each buttie and top with the last slices of buttered bread. Consume with abandon.

4 paua (abalone), about 600 g (1 lb 5 oz) in total
butter, for cooking and buttering the bread
1 loaf of white bread
canola or olive oil, for cooking
1 red onion, sliced into long, thin strips
1 tablespoon crushed garlic
1–2 red chillies, very finely chopped (seeds optional)
1 large handful of fresh coriander (cilantro) leaves, roughly chopped
juice of 1 lemon
4 handfuls of rocket (arugula)

Nothing beats fresh seafood and it doesn't get any fresher than the chef cooking it only 50 metres away from where it was just caught.

Pheasant on couscous with a wheat beer and boysenberry sauce   SERVES 2

Preheat the oven to 200°C (400°F/Gas 6). Wipe the mushrooms with a moist paper towel to clean off any dirt, then put in a roasting tin with the onion pieces. Season with salt and pepper and then drizzle with half the olive oil and put in the oven for about 15 minutes, or until softened.

Remove the breast fillets from the pheasant and the legs and set aside for later. Score the skin of the pheasant with a sharp knife and then season with salt and freshly ground black pepper. Cook in a very hot frying pan with the remaining olive oil, skin side down, until the skin is brown and crisp. You may need to use a spatula to press the breast down firmly to keep all the skin in contact with the pan.

Sprinkle the thyme over the mushrooms and onion, then put the pheasant, skin side up, on top of the thyme and cook in the oven for about 5 minutes, or until cooked to your liking. Remove the pheasant, mushrooms and onion from the tin, keeping separate. Cover with foil.

For the couscous: Bring the water to the boil, add the olive oil, a generous pinch of salt and the couscous. Take off the heat, cover and leave for a couple of minutes. Add the butter to the couscous and mix it through using a fork to separate the grains, then chop the roasted onion and mix it with the lemon zest and parsley.

Put the roasting tin on the stove over medium heat and deglaze it — if there is no juice, you can add a little butter. Fry the shallots in the tin until softened, then add the beer, chicken stock and the boysenberry and garlic sauce. Season to taste and simmer until reduced to about 3 tablespoons or to a consistency you like.

Cut all of the meat away from the legs and then cut that meat into thin strips. Season with salt and pepper and then flash-fry in a hot pan with some olive oil. Add 1–2 tablespoons of the roasted cherry chutney, mix through well and then remove from the heat.

Sauté the spinach with a splash of oil until wilted.

Make a mound of couscous, top with some slices of pheasant breast. Add the mushrooms, wilted spinach and a mound of the leg meat. Serve with the beer and boysenberry sauce and cherry chutney.

4 large Swiss brown mushrooms
1 large red onion, quartered
4 tablespoons olive oil
1.25 kg (2 lb 12 oz) pheasant
1 bunch of thyme
20 g (¾ oz) butter
4 French shallots, peeled
125 ml (4 fl oz/½ cup) wheat beer, such as Emerson's Bavarian wheat beer (see note)
3 tablespoons chicken stock
3 tablespoons boysenberry and garlic sauce (see note)
1–2 tablespoons roasted cherry chutney (see note)
4 large handfuls of baby English spinach

COUSCOUS
250 ml (9 fl oz/1 cup) water
2 tablespoons good-quality olive oil
185 g (6½ oz/1 cup) couscous
20 g (¾ oz) butter
grated zest of 1 lemon
1 tablespoon chopped parsley

There are many brands of Bavarian-style or Hefeweizen beer — Schofferhofer, Erdinger or Franziskaner are just three. As for the boysenberry and garlic sauce and the roasted cherry chutney I'm sure you can find equivalent products at a really good deli or farmers' market.

Acknowledgements

This book could not have happened without the success of my television show, 'Mercurio's Menu'. And 'Mercurio's Menu' could not have happened without the ongoing support of a lot of very talented, committed, hard working and passionate people. I am truly the tip of the iceberg, for underneath the smiling face on TV there are a myriad of people from all walks of life I would like to thank for making the show so great and enabling this book to be.

I would like to thank all of the following: Tim Worner, Brad Lyons and Graeme Hill from Channel Seven for supporting the series, WTFN Productions Daryl Talbot, Steve Oemcke, Frank Dumphy for actually making the show and dealing with all of what that actually means. My crews for the first two series – series one: producer Anne Marie (Sparky) Sparkman, camera man extraordinaire Mick Purdy, sound guy Chris (Pav) Rynn, 2nd producer Damien Estall and for series two: producer Mark (Boomer) Bayly, camera man Mark (Mr Dob Dob) Doberer, camera assist Erin Bishop.

Whilst we are out on the road shooting the show there are multitudes of people back in the office doing all sorts of things to make sure the show is as good as it can be – editors, technicians, marketing, sponsorship, researchers, accounts, management etc the list goes on and on and I would like to say thank you to them all and especially to Julia Nesbit who has headed up the research for MM and made sure things have gone as smoothly as possible when we are out on the road.

A very big thank you to all the chefs I have worked with on the show, it has been a pleasure and an education, I really do appreciate the time and the gentle support you have all shown me. Thanks also to Achim Herterich from Kuche Inspirational Foods for the help he has given me whenever I needed some advice or guidance when developing or perfecting a recipe.

Thanks to Watercooler Talent David Wilson and Malinda Martin for their advice and support and of course my family – my wife Andrea for almost always liking my experiments, my daughter Elise for her expert advice and assistance and my other daughters Emily and Erin whom I love to cook with.

To everyone at Murdoch Books, I thank you for making this book at short order and for doing such a brilliant job.

I couldn't make the show or write a cookbook if we didn't have the wonderful and dedicated people around Australia (and New Zealand) making, growing and nurturing the amazing produce they do. I can't say enough about these people only that it has been my pleasure to have met you all and share in your labours of love, you are all truly inspirational. I look forward to seeing you on the road again soon.

Lastly, thanks to you dear reader for buying this book - that's right, don't put it back down on the shelf and walk out of the store, take it up to the counter, buy it, go home and start cooking. If someone bought it for you as a gift then what better way to say thanks than to cook them a meal.

Cheers!

Index

Published in 2009 by Murdoch Books Pty Limited

Murdoch Books Australia
Pier 8/9
23 Hickson Road
Millers Point NSW 2000
Phone: +61 (0) 2 8220 2000
Fax: +61 (0) 2 8220 2558
www.murdochbooks.com.au

Murdoch Books UK Limited
Erico House, 6th Floor
93–99 Upper Richmond Road
Putney, London SW15 2TG
Phone: +44 (0) 20 8785 5995
Fax: +44 (0) 20 8785 5985
www.murdochbooks.co.uk

Publisher: Jane Lawson
Food Photographer: Stuart Scott
Stylist: Kate Brown
Designer: Hugh Ford
Project editor: Livia Caiazzo
Copy editor: Zoe Harpham
Food editor: Sonia Greig

www.paulmercurio.com.au

Text copyright © Murdoch Books Pty Ltd 2009
The moral right of the author has been asserted.
Food photography © Murdoch Books Pty Limited 2009
Design copyright © Murdoch Books Pty Limited 2009

Cover photography by Amanda McLauchlan
Some photographic images used on pages 156, 157 and 159, copyright Tourism Tasmania, Steve Lovegrove, James Emms,
Holger Leue, George Apostolidis, Geoff Murray, Joe Shemesh, and Don Stephens.

All rights reserved. No part of this publication may be reproduced, stored in a retrieval system or transmitted in any form or by
any means, electronic, mechanical, photocopying, recording or otherwise, without the prior written permission of the publisher.

National Library of Australia Cataloguing-in-Publication Data
Author: Mercurio, Paul, 1963-
Title: Mercurio's menus / Paul Mercurio.
ISBN: 9781741966138 (pbk.)
Notes: Includes index.
Subjects: Cookery, Australian, Cookery, New Zealand, Cookery--Australia, Cookery--New Zealand, Australia--
                 Description and travel, Australia--Guidebooks, New Zealand--Description and travel, New Zealand--Guidebooks.
Dewey Number: 641.5944

A catalogue record for this book is available from the British Library.

PRINTED IN CHINA

IMPORTANT: Those who might be at risk from the effects of salmonella poisoning (the elderly, pregnant women, young children
and those suffering from immune deficiency diseases) should consult their doctor with any concerns about eating raw eggs.

OVEN GUIDE: You may find cooking times vary depending on the oven you are using. For fan-forced ovens, as a general rule,
set the oven temperature to 20°C (35°F) lower than indicated in the recipe.